STORM OVER KABUL

THE HISTORY & TRUTH ABOUT THE AMERICAN LED INVASION OF AFGHANISTAN

By

IMRAN HANIF
MBA, CMgr, FCMI, MIPSA

Copyright © 2015 IMRAN HANIF

The right of Imran Hanif to be identified as the author of this work has been asserted in accordance with the Copyright, Designs and Patents Act 1988.

All rights reserved. No reproduction, copy or transmission of this publication may be made without written permission. No paragraph of this publication may be reproduced, copied or transmitted save with the written permission or in accordance with the provisions of the Copyright Act 1956 (as amended.) Any person who does any unauthorised act in relation to this publication may be liable to criminal prosecution and civil claims for damage.

First published 2015 by Strand Publishing UK, Ltd.
Registered in England & Wales Company Number 07034246
Registered address: Golden Cross House,
8 Duncannon Street, Strand, London WC2N 4JF

www.strandpublishing.co.uk
info@strandpublishing.co.uk

Paperback ISBN 978-1-907340-20-8

Strand non-fiction

Strand Publishing UK Ltd its subsidiaries and associates are not responsible for the statements, views and opinions as expressed in this book as these are purely of the author's.

Acknowledgements

It is with great pride that I acknowledge my own beloved father for his unstinting love and support, also to my wife and daughter for their patience and unwavering belief in me; I extend my sincere gratitude to Dr Zafar Nawaz Jaspal for taking time to critique this book and contribute the foreword - last but not least to my best friend and confidant, my editor, for her fierce loyalty and for trying so valiantly to keep me on the right track.

"I am tired and sick of war. Its glory is all moonshine.
It is only those who have neither fired a shot nor heard the shrieks
and groans of the wounded who cry aloud for blood,
for vengeance, for desolation. War is hell."

William Tecumseh Sherman

This book is dedicated to the people of Afghanistan
who have become one of the most ravaged nations on the planet
due to the longest war in American history;
and to the people of my own dear country Pakistan.

Contents

Foreword 9

Preface 12

Chapter 1 - A Brief History of Afghanistan 17

Chapter 2 - Pak-Afghan Historical Link... 26

Chapter 3 - Osama bin Laden Link... 43

Chapter 4 - Frankenstein Effect 52

Chapter 5 - War Is Hell 73

Chapter 6 - Can The West Win The War In Afghanistan? 86

Chapter 7 - What about Pakistan?.. 91

Chapter 8 - Strategy Debate confusion 98

Chapter 9 - Proxy War 109

Chapter 10 - So What Can The United States of America Do Now? 114

Chapter 11 - New Equations in Afghan Stability 129

Chapter 12 - Way Forward 140

Chapter 13 - Conclusions 158

Some Interesting Facts About Afghanistan 163

About The Author 165

About Dr Zafar Nawaz Jaspal 166

Foreword

Since antiquity the people of Afghanistan have been preyed to the external aggression. Presently, they are suffering from the Great Game(s) of the Great Powers. Indeed, the author of Storm Over Kabul correctly pointed that Afghanistan's geographical location makes it vulnerable to the Great Powers strategic competition for both natural resources as well as political influence in the region. That is why, today, United States, Russian Federation, China, India, Iran and Pakistan are endeavoring to cultivate bilateral strategic cooperation with the current Unity Government stewarded by President Ashraf Ghani.

Storm Over Kabul contains a precise, but an impressive account of Afghanistan's history; the United States military cooperation with the Central Asian States even before the 9/11 terrorist attack; Pakistani intelligence service ISI evolution and its role in Afghanistan affairs in 1980s; and success of the Northern Alliance with the support of the coalition forces against Taliban. It also reveals the secret "Operation Evil Airlift," and contains a detailed review of Osama bin Laden's life as well as his ideological and political philosophy.

The book spells out the interesting diplomatic response by the Taliban Government to the Bush Administration, immediately after Washington's alleging and declaring al Qaeda, led by Osama bin Laden, was responsible for the terrorist attacks in New York and Washington. It explains the reason why the Taliban government refused President Bush's demand regarding the arrest and handover of bin Laden to the American forces. It was stated that bin Laden was a guest in their country and that Pashtun and Taliban codes of behaviour require that all guests be granted hospitality.

Simultaneously, the book highlights Washington's tactics to contain China's role in Asian Strategic Affairs and to encourage India's role in Afghanistan. In addition, it provides detailed discussion on Pakistan and Afghanistan relations that enrich one's understanding on the subject. Moreover, the Taliban and al-Qaeda sanctuaries located in the Federal Administrative Tribal areas and the devastating terrorists' activities inside Pakistan are adequately narrated. It also points out the condemnable role of India's consulates located in the eastern cities of Afghanistan alongside Pakistan's western border. These consulates have been posing a serious threat to the internal security of Pakistan in the form of propagating and supporting sectarian cancer and terrorism menace in the country.

The terrain of Afghanistan is explained in detailed and with a purpose. The terrain is advantageous for the resisting forces, especially in guerilla warfare. Conversely, it was and is very difficult and dangerous for the invaders. Despite the revolution in the military affairs, the technologically advanced armed forces of the former Soviet Union and US/NATO/ISAF coalition has miserably failed in the complex terrain of Afghanistan. The geographical situation compels coalition forces to use drones in many operations to target and kill members of the terrorist syndicate led by al-Qaeda. Nevertheless, the use of drones inside Afghanistan and the tribal areas of Pakistan is counterproductive.

The book contains an interesting analysis of the Afghan's socio-political setup. It points out that the central government in Kabul always lacks its writ in many central and peripheral areas of Afghanistan due to the terrain, fragile road connectivity and tribal culture. The absence of the government authority obliges people living in the rural areas of Afghanistan to give their allegiance to a local clan leader or to a tribal warlord. The local tribal chief/warlord provides protection in exchange for their allegiance. This is an important factor, which maintains the availability of both popular and physical sanctuaries for Afghan Taliban since the demise of their government in Kabul.

The United States Operation Enduring Freedom in the aftermath of the 9/11 terrorist attacks in 2001 will have had a lasting impact on Afghanistan's socio-economic and politico-security affairs. Though, US-NATO led ISAF forces successfully destroyed the al Qaeda sanctuary and network in the country and killed Osama bin Laden hiding at Abbottabad, Pakistan, and dethroned the Taliban leader Mullah Omar from Kabul; yet the mighty military alliance failed to completely destroy the Afghan Taliban fighting potential as well as exterminate the Afghan Taliban's role from Afghanistan society.

Dr. Zafar Nawaz Jaspal
Professor / Director
School of Politics and International Relations
Quaid-i-Azam University
Islamabad, Pakistan

Preface

The story of Afghanistan is in so many ways a very tragic one. Afghanistan is one of the most impoverished nations of the world. It is one of the most war-torn, most ravaged, and most fraught of nations. Since the time of Alexander the Great it is a nation that has been beset by invasion, external pressure and internal turmoil. The people of Afghanistan have endured more than most people can ever imagine. All that has changed in the last few hundred years are the weapons that have been used against so many of them. Whenever I see Afghan people and their sufferings my heart goes out to them.

It is therefore with a heavy heart and great sadness that I decided to write this book about Afghanistan so that people in the West might comprehend, or perhaps become a bit wiser on this issue which has taken so far the lives of countless poor people of not only Afghanistan but also hundreds of European and American soldiers.

My love for Afghanistan and its people developed when I got the chance to serve on the Pak-Afghan borders during my military service, which spanned almost two decades. My interaction with Afghan people motivated me to study and to understand the most important questions namely, why is Afghanistan so important for foreign powers, and why has the country been the victim of the Great Games between the world's super powers?

After having a glance at the regional map of Afghanistan and given a little local knowledge of the region, I suggest that the real reasons for Western military involvement is fundamentally concealed. Afghanistan is adjacent to those Middle Eastern countries that are rich in oil and natural gas and, though the country itself may have little petroleum, it borders both with Iran and Turkmenistan, countries with the second and third largest natural gas reserves in the world. Russia stands in first position.

Turkmenistan is a country nobody even talks about. Its huge reserves of natural gas can only get to market through pipelines. Until 1991, it was part of the Soviet Union and its gas flowed only north through Soviet pipelines. Now the Russians plan a new pipeline north. The Chinese are building a new pipeline east. The United States is pushing for multiple oil and gas export routes. High-level Russian, Chinese and American delegations visit Turkmenistan frequently to discuss energy. The United States even has a special envoy for Eurasian energy diplomacy.

Rivalry for pipeline routes and energy resources reflects competition for power and control. Pipelines are as important today as railway building was important in the 19th century. They connect trading partners and influence the regional balance of power. So Afghanistan is a strategic piece of real estate in the geopolitical struggle for power and dominance in the region.

The United States' main objectives in Afghanistan, to remove the Taliban from power and expel Al Qaeda from the country were their immediate goals in the campaign to defeat terrorism. Part of that campaign was to suppress opium production. Afghanistan produces over 90% of the world's non-pharmaceutical grade opium. It is also the world's main producer of hashish. Profit from the selling of these drugs was, and remains, an important source of funding for terrorists.

The Pentagon and Dr Brzezinski Centre enunciated geopolitical objectives to control the natural resources of Afghanistan and Central Asia to impede the rise of regional hegemonies like Russia or China.

The natural resources of Afghanistan include oil, gas, copper, cobalt, gold, lithium, and other untapped mineral deposits that have an estimated combined worth in excess of a trillion dollars. Among the most strategic of these minerals are rare earth metals, which are indispensable to modern technology. They are needed in manufacturing cell phones, laptops, compact discs, flat screen display monitors, rechargeable batteries, catalytic converters, hybrid cars, and solar panels.

The principal resources of Central Asia are oil, gas, and pipelines. The proposed pipeline is called TAPI, using the initials of the four participating countries (Turkmenistan, Afghanistan, Pakistan and India). Eleven high-level planning meetings have been held during the past seven years, with Asian Development Bank sponsorship and multilateral support (including that of Canada). Plant construction has started but due to various reasons the project is still under scrutiny.

The pipeline project was documented at three donor conferences on Afghanistan in the past three years and is referenced in the 2008 Afghan Development Plan. Canada was represented at these conferences at ministerial level. Thus our leaders must know about it yet they avoid discussion of the planned pipeline through Afghanistan.

The 2008 Manley Report, a foundation for extending the Canadian mission to 2011, ignored energy issues. It talked about Afghanistan as if it were in an island, albeit with a porous Pakistani border. The Prime Minister of Canada Stephen Harper said he, "will withdraw the bulk of the military forces" in 2011, and the remaining troops will focus mostly on, "reconstruction and development". Does that include the pipeline?

The United States involvement in Afghanistan is an example of a great power fighting guerrilla war in pursuit of geopolitical objectives, greater than simply the defeat of a local insurgency. It is the return of the Great Game, where the U.S. and its rivals, Russia and China, seek influence in Afghanistan as a means of securing the resources of Central Asia, in particular, petroleum and pipelines. If the U.S. wins then Russia and China remain lesser powers. If Russia or China win the United States confronts a formidable rival with potential to disrupt the current projection of American power.

Alexander the great took six months to conquer Persia and three years to soothe Afghanistan, a land of dignified and brave people. He wrote to his mother about a country where every foot of ground is like a wall of steel. Many centuries on it was Britain's turn to take on the legendary warrior horsemen. In January 1842, three years after the start of the first Anglo-Afghan war (the present one is the fourth), the stressed British garrison in Kabul, escorting 1500 civilians, began a desperate retreat to Jalalabad. As they crossed the snows of the Hindu Kush, Pashtun tribesmen massacred them all, leaving only one British survivor to tell the story.

In 1979, 30,000 Soviet troops were dispatched to help Kabul's new liberal government fight the Islamist Mujahedeen guerrillas, in whose ranks a young Osama bin Laden was already making a name. The Russians retreated 10 years later with a butcher's bill of 15,000 dead and 65,000 wounded, leaving behind a million dead Afghans. No country as ethnically, politically and religiously fragmented as

Afghanistan, with its warlords, honour codes, Taliban fanatics, suicide bombers and a major illegal source of revenue (opium poppies) could expect an easy ride, but since the Soviet occupation it has not had a single year of peace.

I have tried to make an effort in this small book to bring the Afghanistan issue into the limelight especially for those in the West who have little knowledge, let alone real understanding of the topic. When I ask each of my friends in the United Kingdom why they are fighting a war in Afghanistan, most of them are unable to reasonably answer this simple question?

During my two decades in the armed forces I have spent almost seven years in Baluchistan province (a region equal to 44% of the total area of Pakistan), which is nowadays the centre of attention not only because of its minerals, oil and gas, but due to Gwadar Port which has been built by Pakistan with the support of China.

The port of Gwadar stands just 200 miles from the strategically important Strait of Hormuz, one of the most important oil conduits in the world. Given this, China will have long pondered the possible utility of a port that could shorten its oil transportation chain. If Gwadar port could be developed into a transit facility, or an oil pipeline hub, that would be a major achievement. The robust nature of the China-Pakistan defence ties, and the number of interrelated developments therein, has drawn the port to international attention. China is developing its own western region and has been building a network of roads in Pakistan, and plans to lay pipelines and a railway track. Pakistan offers China a 'trade and energy corridor' via Gwadar linked to inland roads. The plan would see oil being imported from the Middle East, stored in refineries at Gwadar and sent to China via roads, pipelines or railway. Many Western and Indian analysts argue China wants to gain a foothold in Gwadar for such strategic purposes.

In short Baluchistan has a very important role to play, as it links with all three other provinces i.e. Punjab, Sind and Khyber Pakhtunkhwa (KPK). It also shares an 1160km border with Afghanistan, an 832km border with Iran and 560km coastline with the Arabian Sea. Its geographical situation makes it a strategic area.

The Russians fought a bloody war in Afghanistan to reach Gwadar warm water port via Baluchistan. Now the United States along with

NATO forces are at the verge of almost 12 years of war with heavy losses in terms of money as well as human deaths, so things are worse than ever before in the region.

Since I have been monitoring this conflict for a long time I will try to discuss the pros and cons of the complex Afghanistan issue. My efforts will be to present the facts so that people in the West can get to grips with understanding the core issues. I will also try to present a logical conclusion or some kind of way forward, in my humble capacity, with the hope that sense will prevail and an era of peace and stability in the region could start.

Major (Retd) Imran Hanif

Chapter 1

A Brief History of Afghanistan[1]

Afghanistan has historically been the link between Central Asia, the Middle East and the Indian sub-continent. It is a nation made up of many different nationalities – the result of innumerable invasions and migrations. Within its current borders there are many ethnic groups – Baluch, Chahar Aimak, Turkmen, Hazara, Pashtun, Tajik, Uzbek, Nuristani, Arab, Kirghiz, Pashai and Persian. Historically the Pashtun nationality has been the most dominant. When other peoples in the country refer to the Pashtuns they mostly use the word Afghan. The royal families of the country were Pashtun and today the Pashtun represent about fifty per cent of the total population, followed by Tajiks with twenty-five per cent, and the remainder comprising considerably smaller percentages.

Within the country there are small Hindu, Sikh and Jewish communities, but the vast majority of these people are Muslims, and in fact many ethnic groups consider Islam to be one of the defining aspects of their ethnic identity. This is true of the Pashtun for example. The Arabs brought Islam to Afghanistan during the eight and ninth century. Prior to that various Persian, Greek, Sassasian and Central Asian empires had ruled the nation. Following a subsequent breakdown in Arab rule, semi-independent states began to form. These local dynasties and states however were overwhelmed and crushed during the Mongolian invasions of the 1200s, conquerors that were to remain in control of part or all of the country until the 1500s despite much resistance and internal friction. After the fall of Mongol rule Afghanistan found itself in a situation much like in modern times, caught between the vice of two great powers. During this period it was the Mughals of northern India and the Safavids of

---

[1] Based on a speech 'A Brief History of Afghanistan' by Adam Ritscher, delivered to Students Against War teach-in in Duluth, Minnesota (USA) - sourced online and via www.afghangovernment.com/briefhistory.htm.

Iran that fought over the mountains and valleys of Afghanistan. Armies marched to and from devastating the land and murdering the people, laying siege to city after city, and destroying whatever the invading army that preceded it had left behind.

It was not until 1747 that Afghanistan was able to free itself. This was the year that Nadir Shah, an empire builder from Iran, died and left a vacuum in central Asia that a former Afghan bodyguard named Ahmed Shah was able to fill. Ahmad was a Pashtun and his Pashtun clan was to rule Afghanistan, in one form or another, for the next two hundred years. Ahmad was able to unite the different Afghan tribes and went on to conquer considerable parts of what are today eastern Iran, Pakistan, northern India and Uzbekistan. His successors though proved unable to hold his vast empire together and within 50 years much of it had been seized by rival regional powers. Within the country there were many bloody civil wars for the throne and for many Afghans it meant little that their lives were now being uprooted and destroyed by ethnic kin as opposed to foreign invaders.

In the 1800s Afghanistan's internal affairs became dramatically aggravated by the increasing intervention of two new imperialist powers, the British Empire and Czarist Russia. The British were expanding and consolidating their colonial holdings on the Indian sub-continent and identified the Hindu Kush mountains of Afghanistan as a natural barrier to prevent invasion by rival imperialists. The Russians were expanding south and east, swallowing up several formerly independent sultanates and emirates in central Asia; two great powers essentially engaged in a race for Afghanistan. The fiendish seizures of land, overthrowing of indigenous nations, and reckless interference into the affairs of the remaining independent states in the region became known as The Great Game. Imperialists often give such trivial and even vaguely humorous sounding names to their interventionist schemes - but the peoples of the region did not interpret their experience and the consequences of these actions as a game; for them the consequences were devastating. The arrival of European imperialism into the region simply accelerated, and made more devastating, the wars, poverty and material destruction that had already wreaked havoc in the region.

On two separate occasions throughout this period British armies from India outright invaded Afghanistan in attempts to install puppet governments amenable to British economic interests, and that would oppose the economic interests of Czarist Russia. The first, which became known as the First Anglo-Afghan War, took place in 1838. Outraged by the presence of a single Russian diplomat in Kabul, the British demanded that Afghanistan shun any contact with Russia or Iran, and hand over vast tracts of Pashtun inhabited land to British India (regions that are today party of Pakistan). The Afghan ruler Dost Mohammad agreed to these humiliating demands but the British still invaded the country. The British seized most of the major cities in Afghanistan with little resistance but their heavy-handed rule soon resulted in a popular uprising by the people resulting in the massacre of the entire British army of almost 15000.

British outrage over the uninvited arrival of a Russian diplomatic envoy in Kabul forty years later in 1878 resulted in the Second Anglo-Afghan War. Again the British were able to occupy all of the major cities, but unlike the last time, the British got wind of an impending rebellion against their occupation, and brutally crushed it in a pre-emptive move. They did subsequently withdraw but not before they had installed a puppet ruler and forced the country to hand over control of its foreign affairs to Britain. Afghanistan would remain a British protectorate until 1919.

Following the Bolshevik Revolution of 1917 and the subsequent wave of popular rebellions that rippled through Asia, the then king of Afghanistan, Amanullah, declared his country's full independence by signing a treaty of aid and friendship with Lenin and declaring war on Britain. After a brief period of border skirmishes, and the bombing of Kabul by the Royal Air Force, Britain conceded Afghanistan's independence. Stung by this turn of events though, Britain conspired with conservative, religious, and land-owning elements within the country, those people who were unhappy with Amanullah attempting to secularize and reform the country. The consequential uprising and civil war forced him to abdicate in 1929. Different warlords contended for power until a new king Muhammad Nadir Shah took over. He was assassinated four years later by the son of a state execution victim and was succeeded by Muhammad Zahir Shah who was to be Afghanistan's last king and who ruled for the next 40 years.

Like all kings before him Zahir Shah's rule was one of almost total autocratic power. The word of the king was the word of law - while advisory councils and assemblies were sometimes called to advise the king these bodies had no power, and in no way did they represent the people of Afghanistan. These bodies were made up of the country's tribal elders, a rather genteel term that in reality referred to the brutal landowners and patriarchs. Some history books refer to this time of Afghanistan's history as one where attempts were made to 'modernize' the country; all this really meant was newer rifles for the army, the purchase of a small number of airplanes for a token air force, the creation of a tiny airline to shuttle the ruling elite around, and some telegraph wires to allow the king to collect this taxes more promptly. Under his rule political parties were outlawed, and students were shot and killed when they protested.

In 1973 the king was overthrown and a republic was declared but this did little to alter the status quo, for a prominent member of his own family, Daoud, had simply overthrown the king. Daoud decided to title himself president instead of king and under him a certain liberalization took place - meaning that some of the most draconian realities of the monarchy were rolled back but - by and large whatever hopes and expectations arose among the people little was done to satisfy them. Daoud had seized power with the help of an underground party named the Peoples Democratic Party of Afghanistan (DPDA), a pro-Moscow communist party. The PDPA had aided and collaborated with Daoud in exchange for government posts. Once he had consolidated power, and felt he no longer needed these controversial allies, he ditched them and ordered a crack down upon the party.

In 1978 the PDPA seized power from Daoud in a military coup, and after seizing power they began a series of limited reforms, such as declaring, more or less, a secular state, and that women were deserving of equal treatment as men. They sought to curtail the practice of purchasing brides and tried to implement a land reform program. They quickly met with fierce opposition from many sections of the deeply religious population. The PDPA's response to this was very heavy-handed which aggravated the situation, and soon several rural areas rose in open armed rebellion against the new government.

At the same time the party's long history of factionalism came to a bloody head as the more radical wing of the party sought to wipe out those with more moderate tendencies.

Immediately following the PDPA coup, the Soviet Union took an active interest in the so-called socialist revolution unfolding in its backyard. Dismayed by the clumsiness of the radical faction of the PDPA, the Soviet Union invaded in 1979 and handed power over to a man named Karmal, who was the leader of the more moderate faction of the PDPA. Perhaps this was not the Soviets original intent but once inside Afghanistan they found themselves forced to commit more and more troops and material to prop up the unpopular PDPA government. Several Islamic fundamentalist groups sprang up and began waging guerilla warfare, many operating from camps set up by the United States' Central Intelligence Agency (CIA) and Pakistani Intelligence within Pakistan, from which they could strike into Afghanistan, and then beat a hasty retreat over a guarded border. For its part the United States government initially paid little attention to the PDPA coup in Afghanistan. Attention focused instead to the west where a popular revolution had overthrown their most valuable Middle East ally, the brutal and autocratic Shah of Iran.

That all changed once the Soviet Union sent troops into Afghanistan. At that point the United States took an active interest in the Islamic fundamentalists waging war on the PDPA and the Soviets. The CIA began providing military training to the Mujahedeen - the name the Islamic guerillas came to be called. They provided what in the end amounted to billions of dollars worth of weapons, including sophisticated anti-aircraft and anti-tank missiles that allowed the guerillas to take out modern Soviet tanks and jet aircraft.

Year after year, offensive after offensive, gradually the Soviet military became discouraged. They were able to occupy and hold all of the major cities, just as the British imperialists had done the century before, but they were unable to subjugate the countryside. Soviet causalities began to mount dramatically, and with the CIA's providing the Mujahedeen with Stinger missiles, even the Soviet's control of the air was becoming a costly affair.

At the same time the CIA kept increasing and updating the Mujahedeen's supply of weaponry, the Saudis and Persian Gulf

Emirates contributed billions of dollars to their coffers, and thousands of Arabs responded to the Mujahedeen's call for jihad, or holy war, against the secular Soviets - including the wealthy Saudi playboy, Osama bin Laden - who quickly became one of the CIA's most important operatives in its proxy war against communism.

In 1989 the Soviets withdrew from Afghanistan leaving the PDPA government to defend for itself. The CIA soon lost interest in its mercenary forces since they had accomplished their mission of bleeding the Soviets white. Mujahedeen factions began fighting as much among themselves as with the PDPA forces, which resulted in increased suffering and bloodshed. Finally by 1992 Mujahedeen fighters were able to topple the remnants of the PDPA government, bringing to an end the Stalinist's attempts to bring revolution to the people of Afghanistan at the point of a gun.

Mujahedeen warlords then occupied different cities and regions of the country. Burhan-ud-din Rabbani, the same Northern Alliance warlord who recently took Kabul from the Taliban, was the warlord who ruled over the city from 1992 until ousted in 1996. During his reign over 60,000 people were murdered and thousands of women were raped. The current Northern Alliance warlord Rashid Dostum, who is in control of the city of Mazar-E-Sharif, also ruled over the city from 1992, until ousted in 1997. Similarly the warlord Ismail Khan again rules the city of Herat, which he also ruled from 1992 to 1995; and warlord Yunis Khalis is back in control of Jalalabad where he ruled from 1992 to 1996.

So the collapse of the PDPA government did not mark the end of Afghanistan's civil war. The Mujahedeen warlords continued to bring death and destruction upon the country as they fought over the spoils and sought to enlarge their new fiefdoms at the expense of their neighbouring rivals. Meanwhile the CIA having done such a fine job of instigating unrest and warfare in the 1980s appeared indifferent to its aftermath. Pakistani Intelligence forces maintained their interest. Seeking to end the civil war that threatened the stability of their own country (itself a prison house of many nationalities) Pakistani Intelligence aided in the creation of a new Islamic fundamentalist movement, the Taliban[2].

The Taliban was born in the Islamic schools that had sprung up in the Afghan refugee camps inside Pakistan. Its leadership and the bulk of its initial ranks were made up of young religious students, primarily Pashtuns motivated by the zeal of religion and the belief that they were ordained to bring stability and the ways of Allah back to their war torn land. These young men railed against the corruption, greed and factionalism of the contending Mujahedeen factions inside Afghanistan and when they mounted a military push to conquer the country they were initially well received by certain sections of the weary population. Rank and file Mujahedeen fighters and young idealists from inside the country filled their ranks, and city-by-city they were able to occupy most of the country.

In 1996 the Taliban captured the capital city of Kabul, and had forced most of the remaining warlords into a small pocket in the far north of the country. These warlords subsequently formed a defensive alliance termed the Northern Alliance. By the time of the start of the current war, Taliban offensives had reduced their enclave to a mere ten per cent of the country.

Once in power the Taliban sought to create a theocratic state based on their interpretations of the Quran (Holy book). Though already severely repressed by the various Mujahedeen warlords, the plight of Afghanistan's women was made even worse under the new regime. The veil became the law of the land, and women were forbidden from attending school or holding employment outside of the home. Television was banned and an effort was made to purge the country of any signs or remnants of secular or Western influence. The country became politically and diplomatically isolated. Then came the current war.

Following the World Trade Center bombings on 11 September 2001 the United States accused Osama bin Laden of the crime. Bin Laden had left Afghanistan following the defeat of the Soviets but had returned to Afghanistan after falling out of favour in Saudi

---

[2] Taliban – means 'students' [Pashto tlibn, pl. of tlib, *student*, from Arabic lib, from alaba, *to seek*.]

Arabia, and being pressured to leave his first nation of refuge the Sudan. The United States government demanded that the Taliban hand over Bin Laden. The Taliban responded by demanding proof of Bin Laden's guilt, and after receiving no such evidence, they refused to hand him over. Within weeks the United States began bombing the impoverished country as well as providing active support to the Northern Alliance warlords.

Following weeks of devastating bombing, and several failed offensives, the Northern Alliance succeeded in breaking out of its northern enclave, seizing the city of Maser-E-Sharif, and then moving on to take Kabul. This set in motion a series of defeats for the Taliban, which began surrendering and abandoning almost every major city in the country, and retreating into the mountains. The U.S. meanwhile continued its bombing campaign and had Marines on the ground hunting for Bin Laden. All the while the people of Afghanistan continued to suffer.

At that time the United Nations (UN), hardly a radical source of information, estimated that up to 8 million Afghanis could starve that winter due to a shortage of food, made all the more severe by the intentional U.S. disruption of humanitarian aid and bombing of the Red Cross and other humanitarian aid facilities inside the country. U.S. bombs had killed hundreds, and more likely thousands, and many more were dying as the Northern Alliance and Taliban warlords fought it out. Hundreds of thousands of land mines and unexploded cluster bombs lay scattered across the nation's landscape and there was no end in sight to the human misery.

It was hard to say how much longer the Taliban will continue to fight, or when the U.S. would end its war. Afghanistan's future, like its past, looked very dark indeed. Northern Alliance warlords, southern Pashtun warlords, opportunistic émigré politicians, and even supporters of the aging deposed autocrat King Zahir Shah, were arguing about who would be the exploiter-in-chief of this devastated land. It was thought most likely they would come up with some sort of coalition government that would perhaps hold the different factions together, or perhaps not. In the end it mattered little since none of the figures involved represented the people of the country, and none of them ever seemed to have had the people's interests at heart.

So what is the solution for Afghanistan - what will end the suffering of its people? The most immediate thing would be for the United States' government to end its bombing, withdraw its troops completely, and respect the Afghan people's right to self-determination. And while this alone would not end all of the bloodshed and the fighting, it could create a situation where the workers and farmers of Afghanistan would be more able to cast off the warlords and petty feudal tyrants, take control of their own destinies and create a society based upon cooperation and solidarity.

Chapter 2

Pak-Afghan Historical Link

There is a vast corridor along the border between Pakistan and Afghanistan called the Federally Administered Tribal Areas (FATA) of Pakistan. These include seven tribal 'agencies' where about six million of the most independent human beings on the planet live on almost 27,000 square kilometers of rugged and inhospitable terrain. These people are the Pashtuns and they have lived on their lands without interruption or major migration for centuries. They know their neighbourhood very well, and their men have been armed to the teeth since the first bow was strung. Their ancient code involves a commitment to hospitality, revenge, and the honor of the tribe. They are invariably described as your best friend or your worst enemy.

In the 4th century B.C. Alexander the Great fell foul of Pashtun tribesmen in today's Malakand Agency, where he took an arrow in the leg and almost lost his life. Two millennia later the founder of the Mogul empire, Babur, described the tribesmen of the area, now known as Waziristan, as unmanageable. His main complaint seemed to centre on his inability to get them to pay their taxes by handing over their sheep, let alone to stop attacking his armies.

A couple of hundred years later, in the mid 19th century, the British experienced numerous disasters as they tried to bring the same Pashtun tribes to heel, particularly in the agencies of North and South Waziristan. In 1893, after half a century of jockeying for position with Imperial Russia in the aforementioned 'Great Game' the British administrator of the northwest of Queen Victoria's Indian Empire, Sir Mortimer Durand, demarcated the border between India (now Pakistan) and Afghanistan. The Durand line, as it is still known to foreigners (the Pashtuns call it 'zero line' and completely ignore it) separated the tribes on both sides of the line into twenty-six agencies, each with its own laws and tribal councils. It was this area that became the buffer between the British and Russian Empires, an agreed-upon 'middle of the lake'. The tribes were then left mostly to themselves for about eighty years.

There has been no reliable census in the country for decades. The 2010 population is estimated at 29.1 million by the United Nations, with 46 per cent of the population fourteen or younger. Afghanistan is the 42nd largest country by population in the world. Major ethnic groups: Pashtu - 50 per cent, Tajik - 25 per cent, Hazara - 9 per cent, Uzbek - 9 per cent. More than thirty languages are spoken but in the main Pashto and Dari (a Farsi or Persian dialect). Of the country's 99 per cent Muslim population Sunni make up 85-90 per cent or more, and Shia 10-15 per cent. More than five million refugees have returned to Afghanistan since 2002, resulting in a 20 per cent increase in the population. There are still almost three million Afghan refugees, mostly in Pakistan and Iran (about a quarter of the world's refugees). About 300,000 people are internally displaced.

One of the poorest countries in the world, Afghanistan is the lowest-ranking country outside Africa on the UN's human development index. According to the World Bank economic growth will be about 8.5 per cent in 2010-11 and GDP per capita will reach $609, and much of this is aid driven. Unemployment is estimated around 40 per cent. Almost 42 per cent of Afghanistan's population lives below the poverty line. The government's budget for the current year is $4.8 billion, with almost two-thirds going toward military and security spending. By the end of 2009, the international community had pledged over $62 billion in aid since the fall of the Taliban but most of this has not actually been delivered. Afghanistan is the No.1 global aid recipient, receiving about $6.2 billion in aid in 2009, according to Global Humanitarian Assistance. The illegal drug trade worth $2.8 billion in 2009 is equal to one quarter of the GDP, which basically benefits corrupt warlords.

The country's constitution provides for a presidential system, not unlike the U.S., with a House of Elders in place of a senate and the stipulation that the President must be Muslim. The legal system is a mix of civil and Shariah law. The first round of presidential elections was held in August 2009, but massive ballot-box stuffing and other electoral fraud marred them. About one-third of those eligible voted. President Hamid Karzai, seeking a second term, finished in first place with 2.28 million votes, not enough to avoid a second round run-off against Abdullah Abdullah. However, Abdullah withdrew, saying that it would not be a transparent election. The vote was cancelled just a week before it was to take place. Western governments paid the election tab of more than $300 million. The country's previous presidential election was in 2004. After several false starts, Karzai won with 55 per cent of the vote, and the UN reported that three-quarters of the country's eligible voters cast a ballot.

Afghanistan was for a long time a pawn in the so-called Great Game between the British and Russian empires. It broke free of Britain's control following three Anglo-Afghan wars. Afghanistan's descent into conflict and instability in recent times began with the overthrow of the king in 1973. Zahir Shah was in Italy for an eye operation when his cousin, Mohammad Daoud, deposed him in a palace coup. Daoud declared Afghanistan a republic with himself as President. He relied on the support of leftists to consolidate his power and crushed an emerging Islamist movement. It was this that helped lead to a defining moment in Afghanistan's recent history.

Afghanistan was a monarchy until a coup supported by the communists in 1978. In 1979 a faction of the Communist Party carried out its own coup without Moscow's blessing. The Soviet army soon invaded replacing that communist government with one more to its own liking. About a million Afghans lost their lives as the Red Army tried to impose control for its puppet Afghan government. Millions more fled abroad as refugees. Soon after this defeat and withdrawal of the Red Army, the U.S. pulled out all its support and left the country at the mercy of power-hungry warlords. It also left Afghanistan devastated and victim to a series of civil wars, which took the lives of thousands.

Groups of Afghan Islamic fighters, or Mujahedeen, had fought endlessly to try to force a Soviet retreat with much covert support from the United States through Pakistan Inter Services Intelligence (ISI). A ten-year insurgency against the Soviets, supported in large measure by a Cold War-minded Washington, and neighbouring Pakistan, forced the Red Army to withdraw in humiliation in 1989. The Soviet occupation, which lasted until the final withdrawal of the Red Army in 1989, was a disaster for Afghanistan.

When the Soviet Union eventually withdrew they left in power

President Najibullah who had replaced Karmal as leader. He hung on for three years after the Red Army's departure but fell in 1992 as the United Nations was attempting to arrange a peaceful transfer of power. The Mujahedeen swept victoriously into Kabul. After a short interim measure, Professor Burhanuddin Rabbani became president of the new Islamic Republic but his victory was soon soured by infighting as the Mujahedeen factions failed to agree on how to share their new power.

Predominantly rural areas had suffered from the military onslaught during the Soviet occupation as the Red Army tried to flush out the Mujahedeen; but when the Mujahedeen took over it was the turn of urban areas to suffer from the conflict. This was especially true of the capital Kabul, about half of which was literally flattened. Tens of thousands of civilians lost their lives and the country slid more and more into a state of anarchy. Toward the end of 1994 the Taliban emerged in the southern city of Kandahar, the heart of Afghanistan's Pashtun homeland. Their initial appeal and success was based on a call for the removal of the Mujahedeen groups. In 1996 the capital Kabul fell to the so-called hardliners and many say the Pakistan-sponsored Taliban.

After the attacks on the U.S., on 11 September 2001, by Al Qaeda and Osama bin Laden - who had been sheltering in Afghanistan under the Taliban regime - a NATO-led and UN-sanctioned international force ousted the Taliban. The NATO-led force has been fighting ever since, particularly in the south, and in the east along the border with Pakistan. At first they succeeded in gaining control of Pashtun areas with little fighting. Some Mujahedeen commanders defected to their ranks, but as their control spread to other, especially non-Pashtun, regions the fighting intensified and the Taliban went on to control almost 90 per cent of the country.

In 1996 the Taliban captured Kabul and much of the outside world first reacted in dismay at their extreme Islamic policies especially towards the place of women in society. As Taliban control spread the Western world intensified pressure on the Taliban to ban the growth of opium poppies, Afghanistan being the source of most opiates reaching Europe. The United States, in particular, also began their pressure on the Taliban to give up the militant Saudi, Osama bin Laden, whom the Taliban described as their 'guest' in Afghanistan. Washington blamed Osama bin Laden for masterminding the suicide attacks on the World Trade Centre in New York and the Pentagon in Washington on 11 September 2001. The following month the U.S. and its allies began air attacks on Afghanistan, which allowed the Taliban's Afghan opponents to sweep them from power. Kabul was retaken in November and by early December the Taliban had given up their stronghold of Kandahar.

Afghanistan is a landlocked country occupying a strategic position in the region due to its geographical location. Afghanistan has a long experience of power struggles for dominance and has seen many ups and downs in its history. Many nations have exploited the importance of Afghanistan for their own vested economic, military, and strategic interests. Thus the Afghanistan issue is a very complex one, little understood in the West, or not understood at all. The devastation suffered by this nation - if indeed it can be properly called a nation - is unique in history. War has followed war, as inevitably it seems, as day follows night and has resulted in ever-increasing instability in the entire region.

Every invader, from Alexander the Great long ago, to the Americans and their allies today, has discovered that a major factor in any attempted conquest of Afghanistan is the terrain. This is a country of precipitous mountains and deep defiles, of wide rivers, torrents when the rains come, and many nullahs, or small streams. No commander can be unaware of the terrain as a central factor in his strategy. Command and control of the heights is the central factor in frontier warfare as it not only affects observation and survey but also gives psychological ascendancy, no mean factor when troops are under stress in often-severe climatic conditions. Such terrain causes constriction on mobilisation and has channelizing effects. The security of main supply routes is vital for the success of any operation.

Movement in the mountains necessitates decentralization of command and control, and this in turn calls for increased responsibility and initiative, not least at junior officers' level, though in some cases the leaders may be senior non-commissioned officers. Whosoever is the leader, it is clear that looking for orders from central command is not likely to breed any measure of success.

In mountainous terrain there is always an imminent threat of ambush. To prevent ambush, it is necessary to use additional troops in order to protect convoys. And when an ambush occurs, as they so often do, evacuation of casualties, and conversely bringing in additional supplies, can be slow because there is no central command structure.

Although there are rivers and nullahs in abundance, ironically, there can often be a shortage of safe drinking water. The sustenance of soldiers has a direct bearing on the duration of an operation and the military refer to this as the quantum of force. If this were not hard enough, heavy rains can often result in mudslides creating roadblocks that also create problems for routine operational logistics.

Anyone who has tried to use a mobile cell phone in hilly country knows that signal reception can be poor, intermittent, or not available at all. In terrain such as is found in Afghanistan, this question of communication is compounded several times. Mountains and deep ravines screen signals, necessitating support systems for very high frequency (VHF) sets. A patrol that is not only cut off from its company by distance but also by lack of adequate communications systems is always vulnerable.

Of course, the very nature of Afghanistan and the neighbouring regions of Pakistan also have effects on the opposition, the enemy. The very terrain that hampers large troop numbers being deployed then lends itself to the success of small-scale guerrilla operations. There is no better place to hide than in mountainous regions such as Tora Bora[3], as Osama bin Laden proved in the early stages of the

---

[3] Tora bora (Pashto: توره بوره, English: Black Cave), known locally as Spīn Ghar (Pashto: سپین غر, English: White Mountain), is a cave complex situated in the White Mountains (Safed Koh) (Safed Koh is the Dari form for Spin Ghar) of eastern Afghanistan, in the Pachir Wa Agam District of Nangarhar province, approximately 50 km (31 mi) west of the Khyber Pass and 10 km (6.2 mi) north of the border of the Federally Administered Tribal

American attack on Afghanistan, and as the Soviets learned in their ten-year war against the Mujahedeen. And in the dry season what better route to use for infiltration than a dry or black nullah[4]?

In such terrain major roads cannot be constructed in a straight line. Of necessity they must wind through valleys that are themselves dominated by mountain ranges. Thus, there are opportunities in many places for guerrillas to set up an ambush of a military convoy, or a civilian convoy under military protection. In such conditions, roadside bombs have proved most effective.

The terrain affects patterns of habitation. In such country there are predominantly more small villages and hamlets than there are large towns. The Taliban and their Al Qaeda allies gain support from the people of the villages. Indeed, they could not long operate successfully without such support and sustenance. This lesson was learned in Vietnam, and also in the chimurenga[5] the struggle for victory in Zimbabwe. The people of the villages are asked to provide for the Taliban and they do so. They have no choice. So when government or allied troops enter a village, the man who is a Taliban fighter can quickly merge with the population and appear to be a farmer working in his fields.

When politicians and military spokespersons talk rather glibly of winning the hearts and minds of the Afghan people, this fatuous rhetoric is intended for general public consumption both in the United States and in the countries of its many UN and NATO allies. Given the nature of the terrain and the weakness of central government in Kabul, it must come as no surprise to anyone thinking logically that ethnic people will give their allegiance to a local clan leader or to a tribal warlord, for such people provide protection in exchange for their allegiance. It is the social contract in its purest form. Unless you can protect, you will never win hearts and minds.

'In war, truth is the first casualty' - thus wrote Aeschylus the Greek

---

Areas (FATA) in Pakistan.

[4] nullah - A dry riverbed or ravine – a stream.

[5] Chimurenga is a word in the Shona language, roughly meaning 'revolutionary struggle'. The word's modern interpretation broadly denotes a struggle for human rights, political dignity and social justice.

dramatist over two and a half thousand years ago. It was true then and it is true now. Separating truth from propaganda is never easy but this book aims to deduce the facts.

It all started, it seems, (the note of doubt is deliberate) on 11 September 2001, when two aeroplanes were deliberately piloted into the Twin Towers of the World Trade Centre in New York. People all over the United States and in many other countries around the world watched the events as they actually unfolded on their televisions. We were constantly fed re-runs over and over again, filmed from every possible angle, throughout that same day. There was no other news. The United States had been attacked at its very heart.

The story was simple, or so it seemed. Terrorists had hijacked four commercial jet planes and attempted to fly them into several U.S. targets. Whatever one may think about the enormous loss of life, and the destruction of magnificent buildings, one has to admit that the strategy was brilliant and audacious and had been planned with careful sophistication. This was a breathtaking coup, a strike at the very heart of the most advanced and powerful nation on earth. The United States was supposedly dealing with some backward mountain people living in the vastnesses of Afghanistan and Pakistan. Yet now it did not seem so?

The aeroplane attack on the Pentagon in Washington DC resulted in comparatively minor damage; another airliner was brought down in a field by sustained passenger resistance, with total loss of life; but another airliner, American Airlines Flight 11, was deliberately smashed into Tower One of the World Trade Center at 08:50 local time. United Airlines Flight 175 struck Tower Two at 09:04. In under an hour, and as the world watched in horror on screens, Tower Two collapsed to the ground at about 10:00. This scene, unforgettable to those who saw it, was duplicated at 10:30 when Tower One also crumbled and crashed to smithereens. This deliberate attack brought about the death of approximately three thousand men, women and children from many nations around the world, for such is the cosmopolitan nature of New York's population.

The people of America joined together in common outrage, disbelief, and deep mourning. It is hard to grieve for those we do not know, but the graphic pictures shown on television seemed to bring the horror close into the hearts of the American people and their allies in other countries around the world.

How was it possible for two aircraft to penetrate air space right at the heart of the world's greatest commercial city? At few times in their brief history had the American people been so united? This was in many ways a re-run of their feelings following the Japanese attack on Pearl Harbor in 1941, which heralded American entry into World War II. People responded with donations of blood, manpower, and money. Shock and grief were seen clearly on the faces of the American people. President George W Bush immediately called for all civilized nations, as he said, to join together and fight terrorism. The United States military was mobilized for war in an operation called Enduring Freedom, a name with a hopeful and defiant ring to it.

What the president did not tell the world, and dared not tell the world, was that this was no bolt out of the blue. There had previously been attacks on U.S. embassies in Kenya and Tanzania. There had been strikes against the *USS Cole* harboured in the port of Aden on the southern coast of Yemen. There were even rumours of troop movement in countries to the north of Afghanistan, former Soviet republics, and now independent Muslim states striving for independent survival.

The date was 12 October 2000. *USS Cole,* a destroyer under the command of Commander Kirk Lippold, entered Aden harbour for a routine fuel stop. *USS Cole* completed mooring at 09:30 local time. Refuelling started one hour later, at 10:30. At around 11:18 a small craft approached the port side of the destroyer and an explosion occurred, putting a 40-by-60 feet gash in the ship's port side. The blast appeared to be caused by explosives placed against the hull of the boat. At the time there was speculation that more than 1,000 pounds of explosive were used. The blast hit the ship's galley, where crew were waiting in line for lunch, and caused extensive damage. The crew had to fight flooding in the engineering sections. Divers inspected the hull and determined that the destroyer's keel had not been damaged. However, seventeen American sailors had been killed and thirty-nine others injured in the blast. The wounded were taken to the United States Army's Landstuhl Regional Medical Centre near Ramstein, Germany, and were later flown back to the United States. The attack was the deadliest against a U.S. Naval vessel since the Iraqi attack on the *USS Stark* on 17 May 1987.

It was concluded that the attack had been planned, directed, and executed by a terrorist organisation known as Al Qaeda, and that the leader of this group, or network of groups, was Osama bin Laden. A video recording of Osama bin Laden showed him boasting about the success of the attack on *USS Cole*, and encouraged other individuals and groups to plan and execute other attacks on the United States.

The next attack, bigger in scale than *USS Cole*, more adventurous and ambitious, and certainly successful, was 9/11[6]. The people of the United States came together. At least, this was how the media expressed it. The hard truth was that there were already divisions within the United States. Support for President George Bush was not overwhelming. There were deep controversies pervading the country, not least Bush's decision of March 2003 to send troops into Iraq. The reasons given for the invasion of Iraq were clear and commanded much support in the United States and Britain. However countries such as France were lukewarm. President Bush, who as president was also commander-in-chief, claimed that Iraq was developing weapons of mass destruction and also giving aid to Al Qaeda. These allegations were never proved. Indeed, many people came eventually to the conclusion that to invade Iraq and remove Saddam Hussein, the leader of the country, was a monumental error. Saddam was no democrat - no Arab leader ever was; but he was a secularist, and had established control over a diverse and unruly people - Arabs and Kurds - and was no danger to the Western allies.

In Britain, Prime Minister Tony Blair was a fervent ally of George Bush. In wishing to carry the electorate with it, Blair's government peddled lies about weapons of mass destruction. Those who opposed the invasion of Iraq, and there were many - though not among the

---

[6] 9/11 - slang term that has entered common parlance worldwide since the terrorist attack on the World Trade Center, New York, on 11 September 2001. The American Dialect Society, which monitors changes in the English language, declared "9-11" its word of the year for 2001.

main Conservative opposition in parliament - were branded as unpatriotic. In the event, no weapons of mass destruction were ever found, and the electorates of both the United States and the United Kingdom finally reached the conclusion that their respective governments had lied deliberately and had set out to hoodwink. Even the masses of people who find television programmes of utter banality more interesting than politics - more interesting even than the death of soldiers in battle - roused themselves briefly and expressed opposition to the invasion. Opponents of the war in Iraq came from right across the political spectrum and the reasons for their opposition were many.

There was a general viewpoint, however, that the invasion of Iraq was primarily intended for the purpose of gaining, for the Allies, a foothold in the Middle East. More than a foothold, of course: an entire country. Many people felt strongly that attacking Iraq was merely a sideshow, and a deliberate attempt to divert public attention from the real centre of hostilities, which was now in Afghanistan. Since 9/11 there had been a hunt for Osama and his comrades, mainly in the Tora Bora mountain regions. Once the Allies had invaded Afghanistan, the defeat of the Taliban did not take long, as we have noted. The Taliban did, however, re-group and once again become a formidable force - not perhaps in open warfare - for that is rare in any war these days - but in frustrating the Allied efforts to extend full control over such renegade provinces as Helmand.

What was not so quickly concluded was the apprehension and ultimate trial of Osama bin Laden; he eluded capture in 2001 and continued to do so for more than a decade. Capturing Osama would have been a major coup for George Bush, but it was not to be. Indeed, it has never been clear what exactly Al Qaeda is; if it has been established, the definition was kept secret from the people of the United States and Europe. Was Al Qaeda a close-knit group of terrorists led by Saudi Osama bin Laden? Or was it a loose federation of terror groups inspired by, among other motives, extreme Islamist beliefs? One matter was certain: the United States had been attacked on its own soil - at least within its own air space. The federal capital and the main commercial centre had been hit and many lives were lost. Al Qaeda and Osama claimed responsibility for the deadly deeds, which even the enemies of terrorism admit were audacious and successful. One month after the events of 11 September 2001, George W. Bush, President of the United States from 2001 to 2009, identified Osama Bin Laden as the chief suspect in the attacks. Bin Laden was known to be in Afghanistan and Afghanistan had at that time a government led by the Taliban.

If much of what we know of Al Qaeda remains enigmatic and shrouded in mystery, our knowledge of the Taliban is much clearer. It is a political movement with its roots in Sunni Islam, with a tendency to be fundamentalist in its Islamic beliefs, and is composed mainly of men from the Pashtun tribe. This movement is known not to favour education for girls and women, and its members seek stricter codes of law and behaviour, it is claimed, based on Sunni Islam. The Taliban governed Afghanistan from 1996 until 2001, when the swift American-led invasion Operation Enduring Freedom removed it from power in Kabul. From the jaws of what appeared to be utter defeat the Taliban re-grouped and have continued to wage war, often successfully, against the government in Kabul, forces from NATO, (the ISAF), the Americans, and often against neighbouring Pakistan.

So it was in September 2001, while the whole of the United States seemed still in mourning and shock, President George W Bush insisted on several demands that the Taliban government must accept and execute forthwith:
- deliver the Al Qaeda leaders located in Afghanistan to the United States authorities
- release all imprisoned foreign nationals, including American citizens
- protect foreign journalists, diplomats, and aid workers in Afghanistan
- close terrorist training camps in Afghanistan and 'hand over every terrorist and every person and their support structure to appropriate authorities'
- allow access by Americans to training camps, in order to verify their closure

These were harsh demands indeed for any government to make of another sovereign nation - but the times were not normal and, as will become clear, George Bush needed a reason to enter Afghanistan and topple the Taliban, as well as seeking out Osama bin Laden and his associates.

'They will hand over the terrorists or they will share in their fate,' said President Bush, speaking to the American Congress in Washington. 'Our war on terror begins with Al Qaeda, but it does not end there.'

The Taliban government was not one to sit down quietly in the face of such threats, but, knowing the military power of the United States and its allies, it decided to make what was, in the circumstances, quite a conciliatory response sent through the Afghanistan embassy in Islamabad, the capital of Pakistan. There was no evidence of which they were aware that linked Osama bin Laden to the 11 September attacks in America. It was also stated that bin Laden was a guest in their country and that Pashtun and Taliban codes of behaviour require that all guests be granted hospitality. This was probably the first such response in diplomatic history.

On 22 September 2001, the United Arab Emirates and then Saudi Arabia, both of whom had previously recognised the Taliban as the legitimate government of Afghanistan, withdrew recognition - no doubt at the insistence of the American government - leaving Pakistan as the only country with diplomatic ties to the Taliban regime.

On 7 October 2001, before the onset of military hostilities, the Taliban offered to bring bin Laden to an Islamic court in order to assess if he were guilty or not. This offer was rejected. The very same day the United States and British planes carried out bombing raids. The war had started. Nobody believed that it would be 'over by Christmas'[7] though the removal of the Taliban from Kabul was swift and it appeared that the movement had been destroyed or at least dispersed.

What is likely and less well known is that U.S. Army Rangers were

---

[7] One of the most popular sayings at the outbreak of World War II - when war broke out in August 1914, many said that it would be 'over by Christmas'. By the end of the year the high rate of casualties and shocking acts of violence against civilians made it clear that would not be the case.

training special troops inside Kyrgyzstan and there were reports - unconfirmed but likely, given what we know of political and military deceit - that Tajik and Uzbek special troops were being trained in the American states of Alaska and Montana even before the attack on the Twin Towers. The United States was determined to invade, despite their knowledge of the ten year Soviet involvement and ultimate defeat. The Russians had claimed at the time that they were making a tactical withdrawal, but everyone knew it was a defeat.

The initial plan was to attack from the north, from Uzbekistan and Tajikistan. The latter country was deemed to be especially important strategically. The United Nations Security Council did not authorize Operation Enduring Freedom, as the United States grandly and optimistically termed the invasion. According to the Americans, UN authorization for the invasion was not legally required because this was an act of national self-defence and not aggression; but even if UN sanction had been legally necessary, under the UN Charter, the Americans, in belligerent mood, would doubtless have gone ahead anyway. There was no declaration of war. This was an incursion to capture terrorists not soldiers. This being the case, those captured were transferred to Guantanamo Bay, an American enclave in Cuba. The United States had assumed territorial control over the base under the 1903 Cuban-American Treaty, which granted the United States perpetual lease of the enclave. As the detainees sent there from Afghanistan were considered to be terrorists, not soldiers, they did not have the rights and protection afforded to soldiers; they did not come under the provisions and protection of the Geneva Convention.

Two months later, on 20 December 2001, the United Nations Security Council via Resolution 1386 authorized the creation of an International Security Assistance Force (ISAF) with authority to assist the Afghan Interim Authority in Kabul in maintaining, as far as possible, law and order. In December 2001 command of ISAF passed to the North Atlantic Treaty Organization (NATO). This was fictitious - everyone knew that actual control was in the hands of the Americans, the senior partner in any Western alliance. After initial bombing the ground offensive commenced. The first ground troops were from the Central Intelligence Agency's Special Activities Division. U.S. Army Special Forces from the 5th Special Forces

Group soon joined them. These combined groups led the Northern Alliance intending to overthrow the Taliban. This was achieved without the deployment of conventional US forces. Strikes were made on Kabul at the airport, on the city of Jalalabad, and on Kandahar the home of Mullah Omar leader of the Taliban. An attempt was made to soften liberal criticism with an announcement that while the Taliban would be targeted, as would terrorist training camps, at the same time food and medical supplies would be dropped to alleviate suffering by the civilian population of the country.

The declared aim of the invasion was to find Osama bin Laden and other high-ranking Al Qaeda leaders, bring them to trial, and thus destroy the whole organization of Al Qaeda. The secondary purpose was to destroy the Taliban regime, which had afforded safe haven to Al Qaeda. The Bush administration doctrine stated that it would not distinguish between terrorist organisations and nations or governments that harboured them. It was the age-old dictum 'you are either for us or against us'. It seemed there was no place for neutrality.

In a pre-recorded videotape Osama bin Laden was in jaunty mood. He declared that the United States would fail in Afghanistan, just as the Soviets had done earlier. It is on record that bin Laden believed events in Afghanistan had been the prime cause of the collapse of the Soviet Union. The collapse of the United States could also be achieved.

The ISAF was established by the UN Security Council and placed under NATO command. ISAF has more than 130,000 soldiers provided by 50 countries.

ISO Code	COUNTRY	TROOPS end July 2009	TROOPS 6 June 2011
AL	Albania	140	260
AM	Armenia	0	40
AU	Australia	1090	1550
AT	Austria	3	3
AZ	Azerbaijan	90	94
BE	Belgium	510	507

BA	Bosnia & Herzegovina	2	55
BG	Bulgaria	470	602
CA	Canada	2800	2922
HR	Croatia	295	320
CZ	Czech Rep	340	519
DK	Denmark	700	750
EE	Estonia	150	163
FI	Finland	110	156
FR	France	3160	3935
GE	Georgia	1	937
DE	Germany	4050	4812
GR	Greece	145	162
HU	Hungary	310	383
IS	Iceland	8	4
IE	Ireland	7	7
IT	Italy	2795	3880
JO	Jordan	7	0
KR	Korea – South	0	426
LV	Latvia	165	139
LT	Lithuania	200	237
LU	Luxembourg	9	11
MK	Macedonia	165	0
MY	Malaysian	0	31
MN	Mongolia	0	74
ME	Montenegro	0	36
NL	Netherlands	1770	192
NZ	New Zealand	160	191
NO	Norway	485	406
PL	Poland	2000	2560
PT	Portugal	90	133
RO	Romania	1025	1938
SG	Singapore	8	21
SK	Slovakia	230	308
SI	Slovenia	80	80
ES	Spain	780	1552
SE	Sweden	430	500
MK	Macedonia		163

TG	Tonga		55
TR	Turkey	730	1786
AE	UAE	25	35
UA	Ukraine	10	22
GB	United Kingdom	9000	9500
US	United States	29,950	90,000
	TOTAL	64,495	132,457

The ratios remain much the same now, though these ISAF figures are for June 2011[8]. This is a U.S. and British war. The figures make it obvious. Despite all the fiction surrounding ISAF, and despite having been sanctioned by the United Nations Security Council, this is to all intents and purposes an American invasion with the United Kingdom as its principal ally.

Now that Osama bin Laden has been 'found and killed'[9], still many people have little knowledge about this former 'most wanted man on earth'. So who is he, or rather, who was Osama bin Laden?

---

[8] ISAF troop numbers - Available online at http://www.theguardian.com/news/datablog/2009/sep/21/afghanistan-troop-numbers-nato-data

[9] Allegedly on the night of 2 May 2012, Abbottabad, Pakistan by U.S. Navy Seals.

Chapter 3

Osama bin Laden Link

Osama bin Laden was born in Riyadh, Saudi Arabia. In an interview in 1988 he gave his date of birth as 10 March 1957. His father Mohamed Awad bin Laden was a wealthy businessman with ties to the Saudi royal family. Osama was born the only son of Mohamed bin Laden's tenth wife. Soon after the child's birth the parents divorced. The mother then married again and Osama lived in the new household with three stepbrothers and one stepsister.

Bin Laden was raised as a devout Wahhabi Muslim. He studied economics and business administration at King Abdul Aziz University. Reports of his academic achievement vary - some sources claim that he earned a degree in civil engineering in 1979; others state it was public administration and he graduated in 1981. There are also sources that suggest he dropped out in his third year. What everyone appears to agree upon is that while at university bin Laden's main interest was religion.

In 1974, at the age of 17, he married his first wife. Sources vary in respect of his wives and children - some suggest four women and 25 or 26 children, while others talk of between 12 and 24. Whatever the numbers he clearly did not spend his whole time reading within religion.

Bin Laden believed that the restoration of Sharia law[10] would set things right in the Muslim world, and that all other ideologies had to be opposed. He believed Afghanistan, under the rule of Mullah Omar's Taliban, to be the one true Islamic country and had consistently dwelt on the need for violent jihad to right what he believed were injustices against Muslims perpetrated by the United States. Israel needed to be wiped from the map. Gambling, usury, homosexuality, the taking of drugs including alcohol, must not be

---

[10] Sharia - the code of law; in its strictest definition, a divine law, as expressed in the Qur'an and by Muhammad's (pbuh) example.

permitted. Osama was against any form of democracy.

Probably the most infamous and loathsome part of Bin Laden's ideology was that civilians, including women and children, were legitimate targets of jihad[11]. He was anti-Semitic, and had warned against alleged Jewish conspiracies. Nor were all Muslims spared - Shia[12] Muslims have been listed along with heretics, the United States, and Israel as the four enemies of Islam. Music had no place in his worldview, but killing thousands of civilians in the name of jihad was acceptable.

Osama bin Laden had been living in Afghanistan along with other members of Al Qaeda, operating training camps and having an alliance with the Taliban. How strong this alliance was has never been made clear. When, in 1998, U.S. embassies in Africa were attacked, with significant loss of life, notably in Kenya, the U.S. military responded by launching cruise missiles at these camps. How effective these strikes were in terms of limiting Al Qaeda activities is also not known.

Over the next two years the United Nations (UN), (usually a dilatory organisation, a mere talking shop to express it mildly) issued Resolution 1267 (1999) and Resolution 1333 (2000). These resolutions were specifically aimed at the Taliban. Sanctions, both financial and military, were threatened. The purpose was to persuade the Taliban to hand over Osama bin Laden for interrogation and trial in relation to the Africa bombings. It was also intended that training camps in Afghanistan should be closed. If the Taliban failed to arrest Bin Laden and hand him to the United States military, the United States would consider itself at war with the Taliban, or anyone who aided or gave encouragement to Al Qaeda.

In 2001, after 9/11, as the destruction of the Twin Towers became universally known, the United States was at war. Part of the strategy was to use force to remove the Taliban government in Afghanistan –

---

[11] Jihad - (among Muslims) a war or struggle against unbelievers - the spiritual struggle within oneself against sin.
[12] Shia one of the two main branches of Islam, followed by about a tenth of Muslims, especially in Iran, that rejects the first three Sunni caliphs and regards Ali, the fourth caliph, as Muhammad's first true successor.

'regime change' as such strategies became known. If this necessitated giving assistance to the enemies of the Taliban within the country, then so be it. Again, a famous dictum of Realpolitik[13] is brought to mind: 'My enemy's enemy is my friend'. One of the enemies of the Taliban was the Northern Alliance. Due to the great distances involved the United States needed bases close to Afghanistan. These were to be found in India and Russia, and especially in Uzbekistan and Tajikistan. It was from the latter country - a former state of the Soviet Union, now independent - that the U.S. intended to invade Afghanistan. The objectives were simple: to apprehend Bin Laden and his associates, and to effect regime change in Afghanistan. It could not be simpler – yet in the real world of politics, nothing is ever simple. Wars do not solve problems; they produce even more trouble without solving the original issue.

Bombers operating at high altitudes, well out of range of anti-aircraft fire, bombed Al Qaeda training camps and Taliban air defences. During the initial build-up preceding the actual attack there had been speculation in the media that the Taliban might try to use U.S.-built Stinger anti-aircraft missiles. If any of these missiles existed at the time of the air campaign they were never used, and the U.S. did not lose any aircraft to enemy fire. U.S. aircraft, including Apache helicopter gunships, operated with impunity throughout the campaign.

The strikes initially focused on the area in and around the cities of Kabul, Kandahar and Jalalabad. Within only a few days training sites were severely damaged and the Taliban's air defences destroyed. In order to make it difficult for the Taliban to communicate with one another their command, control, and communication targets were attacked. Despite this strategy the Taliban line opposed to the Northern Alliance remained intact. Two weeks into the campaign the Northern Alliance demanded the air campaign focus more on the front lines. Meanwhile thousands of Pashtun militiamen based in Pakistan crossed into Afghanistan to join their fellows. In any event the frontier between the tribal areas of the two countries has never

---

[13] Realpolitik - a system of politics or principles based on practical rather than moral or ideological considerations.

been strongly demarcated due to the terrain.

The next stage of the campaign began with carrier based F/A-18 Hornet fighter-bombers hitting Taliban vehicles in pinpoint strikes, while other U.S. planes began cluster-bombing Taliban defences. The war was well planned and appeared to be going according to plan. Following years of fighting the Northern Alliance smelled success. The Taliban support structure began to erode under the pressure of air strikes. U.S. Army Special Forces judged the time was right to launch an audacious ground raid deep into the Taliban's heartland of Kandahar, even striking one of Mullah Omar's compounds.

At the beginning of November, the Taliban front lines were relentlessly bombed with 15,000-pound bombs and by AC-130 helicopter gunships. The Taliban fighters had no previous experience of such sustained fire power as produced by the Americans, not even in the ten years of Soviet occupation, and they were unsure how to, or if indeed they could, respond. This was a war the like of which the Americans had promised in Iraq, one of 'shock and awe'. By 2 November Taliban frontal positions had been broken and the Northern Alliance was poised to take Kabul.

As the Taliban collapsed, so Al Qaeda fighters took over security in Afghan cities. What made the Afghan campaign a landmark in the military history of the United States was that Special Operations Forces from all the services prosecuted it along with Navy and Air Force tactical power. Other operations by the Afghan Northern Alliance and the CIA were equally important and fully integrated. No large army or marine forces were initially deployed. During these early months of the war the U.S. military had a limited presence on the ground. The plan was that Special Forces and intelligence officers with a military background would serve as liaisons with Afghan militias opposed to the regime, and would advance after air power had destroyed the Taliban.

Intelligence reports identified the Tora Bora Mountains, which lie roughly east of Afghanistan's capital Kabul, itself close to the border with Pakistan, as the place where Osama bin Laden and his commanders were hiding. American intelligence analysts believed that the Taliban and Al Qaeda had dug in behind networks of fortified caves and underground bunkers, and that Bin Laden and his commanders where in one of these caves. The area was subjected to a heavy and almost continuous air bombardment by B52 bombers. To the Northern Alliance it seemed that the main American objective was the capture of Osama and his henchmen, and their subsequent trial. The main objective of the Northern Alliance was to take over the government of the country from the discredited and defeated Taliban.

On 5 November, General Abdul Rashid Dostum, generally accepted as the leader of the Uzbeks living in Afghanistan, and himself a former pro-Soviet supporter in the Russian invasion, led the Uzbek faction in attacking the towns of Keshendeh-bala, Keshendeh-pane and various other strongholds within the Darya Suf Valley south-west of Mazar-i-Sharif, seizing them with the assistance of U.S. Special Operators and with his troops mounted on horse-back.

In the town of Bai Beche the tide began to turn with the death of a key Taliban commander, the capture of another, and the destruction of 150 troops during a battle that lasted twelve hours. At the same time 2000 Tajik forces moved south. On the road to Kabul the city of Mazar-i-Sharif was about to fall. The Northern Alliance feared reprisals[14] at the hands of the Taliban.

Al Qaeda did not sit still. They moved 4,000 fighters across country to organise a defence of Mazar-i-Sharif. The battle commenced with American Special Forces launching precision bombing on selected targets. Those Taliban and Al Qaeda commanders living in bunkers were specifically targeted; even so the Taliban boasted they could hold the city. Mazar-i-Sharif was considered important, not only because it is the home of the Shrine of Azar Ali, or Blue Mosque, a site sacred to Islam, but also it is the location of two airports and a major road that leads into Uzbekistan. The capture of this city was vital to the Allied effort.

On November 9, Northern Alliance forces, under the command of Generals Dostum and Mohammed Door, Uzbek and Tajik respectively, swept across the Pu-i-Imam Buckhorn Bridge meeting little resistance, and seized the city's main military base and airport.

---

[14] This country has over many centuries witnessed savage reprisals - no group or clan has clean hands.

American Special Forces were also in the field. In wars strange bedfellows lie down together against what is perceived to be a common enemy. The fall of the city of Mazar-i-Sharif was swift and soon the Taliban and Al Qaeda were in retreat. The defenders of the city included fighters who were Chechen, Pakistani, Uzbek, Chinese Muslims, and not a few Arabs who had come especially to Afghanistan to defend the country against what they considered were infidel[15] invaders.

Withdrawal from the city began. The Northern Alliance forces entered from the Balk Valley meeting only light resistance. By sunset the majority of the Taliban forces had retreated to the north and east in an attempt to mass for a counter-attack. It was later estimated that 400 - 600 people had died in the battle. Approximately 1,500 Taliban were captured or chose to defect to the opposition. A mere two months since the destruction of the Twin Towers the capture of Mazar-i-Sharif on Friday 9 November represented the first substantial victory of the campaign, and for the Allies it was a considerable propaganda coup.

Taliban officials asserted that they would be able to move 500 fresh fighters into the city. Upholding this assertion as many as 900 Pakistani fighters reached Mazar-i-Sharif in the following days, just as the majority of the Taliban were evacuating. It was claimed later that many of these young men were recruited by a Pakistani Mullah, Sufi Mohammed, who used a loudspeaker riveted to a truck to broadcast 'Those who die fighting for God don't die! Those who go on jihad live forever, in paradise!'

For almost two days as the group, led by a large number of Chechen and Arab sympathisers, gathered in the abandoned Sultan Razia Girls' School building. It is somewhat ironic that a government so fiercely opposed to the education and advancement of females should make a stand in a girls' school. Town officials and leaders of the Northern Alliance attempted negotiations for their surrender, but the fighters vehemently refused, ultimately killing the representatives including two peace envoys, a town mullah and his military escort. All

---

[15] infidel (n) one who has no religion or whose religion is not that of the majority.

the while they constantly fired at anyone who moved within the vicinity of the building, including civilians drawn to the scene out of curiosity and for several it was to be lethal. After the murders of the envoys the Northern Alliance began returning fire on the school but with little immediate effect. This gun battle continued for several hours. Inside the battered school, someone scrawled on the walls the words of their mullah: 'Die For Pakistan' and 'Never Surrender'. By mid-afternoon it had been decided to dislodge the defenders by bombing them - planes were called in and the compound obliterated.

The capture, occupation and holding of Mazar-i-Sharif had significant strategic importance. Supply routes were again open; there was an airstrip for humanitarian aid via U.S. airlifts as well as deliveries by relief organizations to hungry people in the countryside. This aid alleviated Afghanistan's looming food crisis, which had threatened more than six million people with starvation. A large proportion of those in most urgent need lived in rural areas to the south and west of the city.

Then rumours started to circulate that Mullah Dadullah was moving towards Mazar-i-Sharif in command of 8,000 Taliban soldiers. Dadullah was a Pashtun and senior military commander of the Taliban until his death in 2007 at the age of about forty-one. He was a handsome and charismatic commander with several victories to his credit. In response to this very real threat one thousand American troops were rushed to the defence of the city. Now the Americans had their own air base from which to launch air strikes; formerly they had to scramble flights from as far away as Uzbekistan or from aircraft carriers in the Arabian Sea (that warm water that the Tsars had so coveted) with the Soviets after them. The expected counter-offensive did not materialise though Mullah Dadullah continued to lead a busy and often brutal life. It is worth noting that Dadullah had lost a leg fighting with the American-supported Mujahedeen against Soviet occupation in the 1980s. Before the American invasion in 2001, the year that the country joined the Great Game, Dadullah had been on the central council of the Taliban, in effect the parliament of Afghanistan; not that the Taliban would have set up anything resembling a western-style parliament.

The American-backed forces now controlling the city began

broadcasting music; the Taliban had banned all music for the previous five years. A female announcer introduced the songs. This was another major breakthrough for women had, since 1996, been prohibited from education, work, and many other civil liberties, even the most basic kind. This in stark contrast to the West, where the advancement of women has in recent years been rapid, to the extent that women occupy positions of power such as the UK's former Prime Minister Margaret Thatcher, Germany's Chancellor Angela Merkel, and U.S. Secretary of State Condoleezza Rice. The Taliban wanted a return to feudal times indeed much of the ideological thinking of extreme Muslims has a medieval cast.

The capital Kabul was the next city to fall. On the night of 12 November, Taliban forces fled from the city leaving under the cover of darkness. By the time Northern Alliance forces arrived in the afternoon of 13 November, only bomb craters and destroyed gun emplacements were there to greet them but there was a group of about twenty hard-line Arab fighters hiding in the city's park. All members of this group were killed in a fifteen-minute gun battle. So the capital was secured. Mullah Dadullah had escaped to carry on the fight in another way and on another day, which he assuredly did.

Dadullah had been a central figure in the recruitment of Pakistani nationals to the Taliban, and was also one of the main Taliban spokesmen frequently meeting Al-Jazeera television reporters. In the summer of 2006 he was reportedly sent by Mullah Omar to South Waziristan to convince local Pashtun insurgents to agree a truce with Pakistan. It was even rumoured that in 2006, as part of a deal for reconciliation, Dadullah (a man who had instigated the capture and murder of hostages) would be made Minister of Defence. All he had to do was come in from the cold. It was not his destiny, as in May 2007 Mullah Dadullah was killed after a raid on his headquarters. Afghan and NATO troops were involved, also a British unit known as the Special Boat Squadron (SBS) who at the time were operating in Helmand province. Dadullah's younger brother succeeded him as military leader of the Taliban.

The fall of Kabul would surely have marked the collapse of the Taliban. It was widely believed that they could not possibly re-group as a strong fighting force; but alas this was not the case. The return to the battle of the Taliban has been perhaps the major surprise of the whole campaign. Within twenty-four hours of the fall of Kabul to NATO and Northern Alliance troops all of the Afghan provinces along the Iranian border including the key city of Herat had fallen. Local Pashtun commanders and warlords had taken over throughout north-eastern Afghanistan, including the key city of Jalalabad. Taliban numbering 10,000 led by foreign fighters and aided by Pakistani volunteers, fell back on the northern town of Kunduz, and continued to put up resistance refusing to surrender.

Meanwhile American Special Forces scoured the caves of the Tora Bora complex but failed to find Osama bin Laden. Had he been captured this would have been a major coup for the Americans but it was not to be. The war continued with the Taliban recovering quickly and again joining the fight. There were successes for the Allies. The Al Qaeda leader Mohammad Atef was killed in an air strike in November 2001, and this attack also killed other high-ranking Al Qaeda personnel.

At the same time as the bombardment at Tora Bora was increasing, the siege of Kunduz was continuing. Finally after nine days of heavy fighting and heavy American aerial bombardment Taliban fighters surrendered to Northern Alliance forces on 25-26 November. Shortly before the surrender Pakistani aircraft had arrived, ostensibly to evacuate a few hundred intelligence and military personnel who had been in Afghanistan prior to the U.S. invasion for the purpose of aiding the Taliban's ongoing fight against the Northern Alliance. Allegedly up to 5,000 people were airlifted from this region, including Taliban and Al Qaeda troops allied to the Pakistanis in Afghanistan. This operation remains a mystery, and it is doubtful if more than a few individuals know the true story. What is certainly true is that the Pakistan Inter-Services Intelligence (ISI) was deeply involved; but who or what is the ISI? What is the history and what is the true purpose of this branch of Pakistan security?

Chapter 4

Frankenstein Effect

After independence in 1947, two new intelligence agencies were created in Pakistan: the Intelligence Bureau (IB) and the Military Intelligence (MI). Weak performance by the MI in sharing intelligence between the Army, Navy and Air Force during the Indo-Pakistani War of 1947 led to the creation of the Directorate for Inter-Services Intelligence (ISI) in 1948. The ISI was structured to be manned by officers from the three main military services and to specialize in the collection, analysis and assessment of external intelligence, either military or non-military. The ISI was the brainchild of Australian-born British Army officer, Major General R. Cawthorn, and then Deputy Chief of Staff in the Pakistan Army. Initially the ISI had no role in the collection of internal intelligence, with the exception of the North-West Frontier Province and Azad Kashmir. The objective of ISI from the beginning was to:

- safeguard Pakistani interests and national security inside and outside the country.
- monitor the political and military developments in adjoining countries, which have direct bearing on Pakistan's national security and in the formulation of its foreign policy and to collect foreign and domestic intelligence in such cases.
- co-ordinate the intelligence functions of the three military services.
- keep vigilant surveillance over its cadre, foreigners, the media, politically active segments of Pakistani society, diplomats of other countries accredited to Pakistan and Pakistani diplomats serving outside the country.

In the late 1950s when Ayub Khan became the President of Pakistan he expanded the role of ISI in safeguarding Pakistan's interests, monitoring opposition politicians and sustaining military rule in Pakistan. The ISI was reorganised in 1966 after intelligence failures in the Indo-Pakistani War of 1965, and then expanded in 1969. Khan entrusted the ISI with responsibility for the collection of internal political intelligence in East Pakistan. Later on, during the nationalist revolt in Baluchistan in the mid 1970s, the ISI was tasked with performing a similar intelligence gathering operation.

The ISI lost its importance during the regime of Zulfiqar Ali Bhutto, who was very critical of its role during the 1970 general elections, which triggered the events leading to the partition of Pakistan and the emergence of Bangladesh. After General Zia ul-Haq seized power in July 1977, the ISI was expanded by making it responsible for the collection of intelligence about the Sindh based Communist party and various political parties such as Bhutto's Pakistan Peoples Party (PPP).

The Soviet-Afghan war of the 1980s saw the enhancement of the covert action capabilities of the ISI by the United States Central Intelligence Agency (CIA). A special Afghan Section was created under the command of Colonel Mohammed Yousaf to oversee the coordination of the war. A number of officers from the ISI's Covert Action Division received training in the US and many covert action experts of the CIA were attached to the ISI to guide it in its operations against the Soviet troops by using the Afghan Mujahideen.

One of the least discreditable actions of the Americans, in league with ISI, was to allow the evacuation of Taliban, Al Qaeda and others from Afghanistan to Pakistan when Kunduz was about to fall to the Northern Alliance. This was in November 2001.

Victorious Northern Alliance troops swept into Kunduz shooting wounded prisoners and leaving them to die in the city's marketplace as they ended a two-week resistance by Taliban forces in their last stronghold in northern Afghanistan. Hopes of a peaceful end to the standoff were shattered as Northern Alliance soldiers embarked on house-to-house searches looking for hidden Taliban forces. Up to 5,000 Taliban fighters were said to have surrendered, some of who were hauled away in trucks with their arms tied behind their backs with scraps of cloth. In scenes that fed criticisms of the Northern Alliance and of Washington's support for them, the fly-covered bodies of three Afghan Taliban fighters were left on empty stalls in Kunduz's marketplace. Residents claimed the men were captured after they were wounded in fighting and, contrary to all rules of war, shot dead by Northern Alliance soldiers.

Yet it has been claimed that there was an accord between the

Taliban and the Northern Alliance for Taliban forces to submit peacefully. Under the accord the Afghan Taliban were supposed to have been granted an amnesty. If this is true, and there is no reason to doubt this, it seems that the Northern Alliance was more bent on revenge than on accord. Foreign fighters, mainly Pakistani, Chechens and Saudis, were to be imprisoned and put on trial. The Northern Alliance defended its conduct saying that its forces met resistance as they entered the city. Fierce fighting broke out at daybreak as the main contingent of Alliance troops entered the city. It would appear that Taliban forces ambushed the Alliance soldiers with gunfire and rocket-propelled grenades. Thousands of Alliance troops rushed into the city streets and fought back. What followed was carnage and their claim of one hundred dead Taliban seems to have been a deliberate underestimation. Critics of the Northern Alliance, who see it as a brutal organisation with no interest in bringing together Afghanistan's rival ethnic groups, described this as a massacre. Vengeful reprisals and the scenes of violence gave way to jubilation as the Alliance celebrated the capture of Kunduz following a fortnight siege. Some observers said the city's defenders, including foreign volunteers expecting to fight to the death, were laying down their weapons.

A correspondent for the UK newspaper *The Guardian* reported on 16 November 2001, how 'richly ironic that the first achievement of the war on terrorism has been to install in Kabul the Northern Alliance, for whom terrorism has been the entire line of business and way of life for more than 20 years'.

At a press conference in Kabul, the Northern Alliance said that it now controlled the city of Kunduz but was still facing 'pockets of resistance' to the west. Thousands of Taliban soldiers and Arab fighters were giving themselves up said Abdullah Abdullah the Alliance foreign minister. 'In one area there are 2,000 Taliban including foreigners who have surrendered to the joint commission', he said. 'They left behind their tanks and heavy armour and surrendered their weapons'.

Ali Razim, an adviser to the Alliance commander General Rashid Dostam, said that 5,000 Taliban had eventually surrendered to his forces. Most were locals who were released - but 750 Taliban, who were suspected of being foreigners, were imprisoned at General

Dostam's base near Mazar-i-Sharif. A group of Arab supporters of Osama bin Laden were reported to have broken out of Kunduz and fled to the nearby town of Chardara, just west of Kunduz. The Alliance claimed that they were encircled with nowhere to run.

The fall of Kunduz, after a siege lasting three weeks, ended - at least for the time being - the Taliban's presence in northern Afghanistan and allowed American bombers to concentrate their fire power on Mullah Omar's stronghold of Kandahar. A spokesman for the Pakistan foreign ministry, Aziz Ahmed Khan, said that prisoners who surrender should be treated in accordance with international law. He said Pakistan had asked the UN and the Red Cross to try to establish whether there were any Pakistanis among the dead in Mazar-i-Sharif.

Truth is indeed the first casualty of war. What was not known at the time, save but to a few, was that the Americans had connived with Pakistan to allow the escape of several Taliban and Al Qaeda notables and fighters. This appears to have been at the behest of General Pervez Musharaff, President of Pakistan at that time. The original request by General Musharraf was made to President George Bush, but Dick Cheney the gung-ho vice-president took charge. The approval was not shared out with anyone until well after the event, not even with Secretary of State Colin Powell. President Musharraf said that Pakistan needed to save its dignity and its valued people.

Two planes were involved. These two planes made several sorties per night over a time period of several nights. They took off from air bases in Chitral and Gilgit in Pakistan's northern areas, and landed in Kunduz, where the evacuees were waiting on the tarmac. Certainly hundreds, perhaps as many as one thousand people, actually escaped. Hundreds of ISI officers, Taliban commanders, and foot soldiers belonging to the IMU[16] and Al Qaeda personnel boarded the planes. American officers watching from surrounding high ground dubbed this evacuation Operation Evil Airlift. A senior American diplomat later claimed that Musharaff had fooled the United States. This was

---

[16] IMU - Islamic Group of Uzbekistan: a terrorist group of Islamic militants formed in 1996.

not pursued further. At the time nobody wanted to hurt Musharraf as his prestige with the Pakistan army was at stake.

The real question is why Musharraf did not get his men out before. The ISI, or so it appeared, was running its own war against the Americans and did not want to leave Afghanistan until the last moment. Some have suggested that President Musharraf gained American support for the airlift by warning that the humiliation of losing hundreds perhaps thousands of Pakistani army men and intelligence operatives would jeopardize his political survival. Musharaff was America's man, it seemed, and there was great willingness to assist him. Many of the people evacuated were those Taliban leaders who Pakistan hoped could play a role in a post war Afghan government. In the game of political poker this was a strong card in Musharraf's hand, hence the secret evacuation. No one should ever be surprised at the chicanery of politicians.

By the very nature of such operations it is difficult to cite actual evidence. It is even harder to arrive at the full truth. For those who wish to delve deeper the following secondary sources may be of assistance: *Newsweek* 16 Nov 2001 and 11 Aug 2002; *Los Angeles Times* 16 Nov 2001; *New York Times* 30 Sept 2002; Michel Chossudovsky of the Centre for Research on Globalization[17]. *The Times of India* went even further suggesting on 24 January 2002 that it was not Taliban and Al Qaeda moderates who might be expected to participate in a government of national reconciliation in Afghanistan but the hard core of these two allied movements.

While there may be truth that President Musharaff wanted to get his ISI people out safely there is a tendency to accept the 'right royal cock-up' theory. Such was the tumult of those nights that Taliban and Al Qaeda people found places on the aircraft, not because of some dire plot in Islamabad, but simply because of the confusion that prevailed. On 25 November, the day that Taliban fighters holding out in Kunduz surrendered and were being herded into the Qala-i-Janghi

---

[17] Archive of CRG Articles by Michel Chossudovsky. The URL of this article is: http://globalresearch.ca/articles/CHOARC306A.html. BOOKS. War and Globalisation; The Truth behind September 11, Global Outlook, Shanty Bay, Ont., 2002.

fortress near Mazar-i-Sharif, a few Taliban attacked some Northern Alliance guards, taking their weapons and opening fire. This incident soon triggered a widespread revolt by 300 prisoners who soon seized the southern half of the complex (once a medieval fortress) including an armoury stocked with small arms. Johnny Spann, an American CIA operative, who had been interrogating prisoners, was killed. His death marked the first American combat death in the war.

The revolt was finally put down after seven days of heavy fighting between an SBS unit along with some U.S. Army Special Forces and Northern Alliance, AC-130 gunships, and other aircraft took part providing strafing[18] fire on several occasions, as well as a bombing air strike. Of the Taliban, 86 prisoners survived, and around 50 Northern Alliance soldiers were killed. Quashing of the revolt marked the end of the combat in northern Afghanistan, where local Northern Alliance warlords were now firmly in control.

By the end of November, Kandahar, the movement's birthplace, was the last remaining Taliban stronghold and was coming under increasing pressure. Nearly 3,000 tribal fighters, led by Hamid Karzai, a westernised and polished loyalist of the former Afghan king, and Gul Agha Sherzai, the governor of Kandahar before the Taliban seized power, together put pressure on Taliban forces from the east and cut off the northern Taliban supply lines to Kandahar. The threat of the Northern Alliance loomed in the north and northeast. Meanwhile, the first significant U.S. combat troops had arrived. Nearly 1,000 Marines, ferried in by CH-53E Super Stallion helicopters, set up a Forward Operating Base (FOB) known as Camp Rhino in the desert south of Kandahar on 25 November. This was the coalition's first strategic foothold in Afghanistan, and was the stepping-stone to establishing other operating bases.

The first significant combat involving U.S. ground forces occurred a day after Rhino was captured when 15 armoured vehicles approached the base and were attacked by helicopter gunships, destroying many of them. Meanwhile, air strikes continued the

---

[18] strafing - attack repeatedly with bombs or machine-gun fire from low-flying aircraft.

pounding of Taliban positions inside the city, where Mullah Omar was holed up. Omar, the Taliban leader, remained defiant despite the fact that his movement only controlled four out of the 30 Afghan provinces by the end of November. As commanders in tight corners do, he called on his forces to fight to the death.

As the Taliban weakened, so the American focus homed in on the Tora Bora. Local tribal militias, numbering over 2,000 strong and paid and organized by Special Forces and CIA paramilitaries, continued to mass for an attack as heavy bombing continued of suspected Al Qaeda positions. 100-200 civilians were reported killed when 25 bombs struck a village at the foot of the Tora Bora and White Mountains region. On 2 December a group of 20 U.S. Commandos was inserted by helicopter to support the operation. On 5 December Afghan militia wrested control of the low ground below the mountain caves from Al Qaeda fighters and set up tank positions to blast enemy forces. The Al Qaeda fighters withdrew with mortars, rocket launchers, and assault rifles to higher fortified positions and dug in for the battle.

By 6 December Omar finally began to signal that he was ready to surrender Kandahar to tribal forces. His forces had been broken by heavy U.S. bombing and he living constantly on the run within Kandahar to prevent himself from becoming a target. In such circumstances, even Mullah Omar's morale lagged. Recognizing that he could not hold on to Kandahar much longer, he began signalling a willingness to enter into negotiations to turn the city over to the tribal leaders, assuming that he and his top men received some protection. The U.S. government rejected any amnesty for Omar or any Taliban leaders.

On 7 December Mullah Mohammad Omar slipped out of the city of Kandahar with a group of his hardcore loyalists and moved northwest into the mountains of Uruzgan Province, reneging on the Taliban's promise to surrender their fighters and their weapons. He was last reported seen driving off with a group of his fighters on a convoy of motorcycles. Other members of the Taliban leadership fled into Pakistan through the remote passes of Paktia[19] and Paktika[20]

---

[19] Paktia (Persian and Pashto: پاکتي) Paktia is basically Pashtia (پښتیا).

Provinces. So Kandahar the last Taliban-controlled city had fallen and the majority of the Taliban fighters had disbanded. The border town of Spin Boldak was surrendered on the same day, marking the end of Taliban control in Afghanistan. The Afghan tribal forces under Gul Agha seized the city of Kandahar while American Marines took control of the airport outside and established the U.S. base.

Al Qaeda fighters were still holding out in the mountains of Tora Bora, while an anti-Taliban tribal militia steadily pushed bin Laden back across the difficult terrain, supported by powerful air strikes guided in by U.S. and UK Special Forces. Facing defeat the Al Qaeda forces agreed to a truce to give them time to surrender their weapons. The truce was later understood to be a ruse allowing important figures including Osama bin Laden to escape. The Allies closed all roads except one and that allowed a walk of about eight to ten hours to the border with Pakistan. It is highly likely that Osama walked this road.

On 12 December fighting flared again, probably initiated by a rear guard buying time for the main force's escape through the White Mountains into the tribal areas of Pakistan. Once again tribal forces backed by British and U.S. special operations troops and air support pressed ahead against fortified Al Qaeda positions in caves and bunkers scattered throughout the mountainous region. By 17 December, the last cave complex had been taken and their defenders overrun. A search of the area by U.S. and UK forces continued into January, but no sign of bin Laden or the Al Qaeda leadership emerged. It is almost unanimously believed that they had already

---

Some Pashtun scholars claim the word Pashtu stems from Pashtia (پښتو = پښتیا), is one of the thirty-four Provinces of Afghanistan in the east of the country. Its capital is Gardez. Area: 6,432 km².

[20] Paktika (Persian/Pashto: پکتیکا) is one of the 34 provinces of Afghanistan. It is in the south-east of the country and maintains a traditional Pashtun tribal social structure. Paktika holds the reputation as being one of Afghanistan's most conservative provinces next to Helmand. Most of the population consists of Sunni Muslim Pashtuns. Its capital is Sharana. Area: 19,482 km².

slipped away into the tribal areas of Pakistan to the south and east. An estimated 200 Al Qaeda fighters were killed during the battle, along with an unknown number of anti-Taliban tribal fighters. No U.S. or UK deaths were reported.

Meetings of various Afghan leaders were organized by the United Nations Security Council and took place in Germany. The Taliban were not included. These meetings produced an interim government and an agreement to allow a UN peacekeeping force to enter Afghanistan. The UN Security Council resolutions of 14 November 2001 included: 'Condemning the Taliban for allowing Afghanistan to be used as a base for the export of terrorism by the Al Qaeda network and other terrorist groups and for providing safe haven to Osama bin Laden, Al Qaeda and others associated with them, and in this context supporting the efforts of the Afghan people to replace the Taliban regime'; and the UN Security Council resolution 20 December 2001: 'Supporting international efforts to root out terrorism, in keeping with the Charter of the United Nations, and reaffirming also its resolutions 1368 (2001) of September 12, 2001, and 1373 (2001) of September 28, 2001'.

Before the U.S.-led invasion, there were fears that the invasion and resultant disruption of services would cause widespread starvation and refugees. The United Nations World Food Programme temporarily suspended activities within Afghanistan at the beginning of the bombing attacks but resumed them after the fall of the Taliban. It was estimated that the productive valleys could, in the absence of hostilities, produce up to 30,000 tons of cereals annually. By 1 November U.S. C-17s flying at 30,000 feet (10,000 metres) had dropped 1,000,000 food and medicine packets marked with an American flag.

After Tora Bora U.S. forces and their Afghan allies consolidated their position in the country. Following a Loya Jirga[21] of major Afghan factions, tribal leaders and former exiles, an interim Afghan

---

[21] Loya Jirga (Pashto: لويه جرګه) - a grand council or grand assembly used to resolve political conflicts or other national problems; Jirga - a Pashto term for a decision making assembly of male elders; most criminal cases are handled by a tribal Jirga rather than by laws or police.

government was established in Kabul under Hamid Karzai. U.S. forces established their main base at Bagram airbase just north of Kabul. Kandahar airport also became an important U.S. base area. Several outposts were established in eastern provinces to hunt for Taliban and Al Qaeda fugitives. The number of U.S-led coalition troops operating in the country would eventually grow to over 10,000.

Meanwhile, the Taliban and Al Qaeda had not yet given up. Al Qaeda forces began regrouping in the Shahi-Kot Mountains of Paktia province throughout January and February 2002. A Taliban fugitive in Paktia province, Mullah Saifur Rehman, also began reconstituting some of his militia forces in support of the anti-U.S. fighters. They totalled over 1,000 by the beginning of March 2002. The intention of the insurgents was to use the region as a base area for launching guerrilla attacks and possibly a major offensive in the style of the Mujahedeen who battled Soviet forces during the 1980s.

U.S. allied to Afghan militia intelligence sources soon picked up on this build-up in Paktia province and prepared a massive push to counter it. On 2 March 2002 U.S. and Afghan forces launched an offensive on Al Qaeda and Taliban forces entrenched in the mountains of Shahi-Kot southeast of Gardez. The jihadist forces, which used small arms, rocket-propelled grenades, and mortars, were entrenched in caves and bunkers in the hillsides at an altitude that was largely above 10,000 feet (3,000 metres.) They used hit and run tactics, opening fire on the U.S. and Afghan forces and then retreating into their caves and bunkers to weather the return fire and persistent U.S. bombing raids. To render much worse the situation for the coalition troops, U.S. commanders initially seriously underestimated the Taliban and Al Qaeda forces as a last isolated pocket numbering fewer than 200. It turned out that the guerrillas numbered between 1,000-5,000 according to some estimates and that they were receiving reinforcements, not least sympathisers from Pakistan and some of the old Soviet republics.

By 6 March eight Americans and seven Afghan soldiers had lost their lives and reportedly 400 opposing forces had also been killed in the fighting. The coalition casualties stemmed from a friendly fire incident that killed one soldier, the downing of two helicopters by rocket-propelled grenades, and small arms fire that killed seven soldiers, and the pinning down of U.S. forces being inserted into what was code-named Objective Ginger resulting in dozens of wounded. However, several hundred guerrillas escaped the dragnet and headed to the Waziristan tribal areas across the border into Pakistan.

During Operation Anaconda and other missions throughout 2002 and 2003 Special Forces from several western nations were also involved in operations. These included the Australian Special Air Service Regiment, the Canadian Joint Task Force 2, the German KSK, the New Zealand Special Air Service and Norwegian Marinejegerkommandoen. Following the battle at Shahi-Kot it is believed that the Al Qaeda fighters established sanctuaries among tribal protectors in Pakistan from which they regained their strength and by the summer months of 2002 began launching cross-border raids on U.S. forces. Guerrilla units numbering between 5 and 25 men regularly crossed the border from their sanctuaries inside Pakistan to fire rockets at U.S. bases, and ambush American convoys and patrols, as well as Afghan National Army troops, Afghan militia forces working with the U.S-led coalition, and non-governmental organizations (NGOs). The area around the U.S. base at Shkin in Paktika province saw some of the heaviest activity.

Taliban forces remained in hiding throughout the rural regions of the four southern provinces that formed their heartland Kandahar[22], Helmand[23], Uruzgan[24] and Zabul[25]. In the wake of Operation

---

[22] Kandahar or Qandahar, (in older literature Candahar) the second largest city in Afghanistan with a population of about 512,200 as of 2011.

[23] Helmand or Hillmand – (hel-mund; Pashto/Balochi: هلمند) is one of the 34 provinces of Afghanistan, located in the south of the country. It is one of the largest, covering 58,584 square kilometres area - Area: 58,584 km².

[24] Uruzgan also Oruzgan – (Pashto: ارزروز or ارزگاناوروز) - one of the thirty-four provinces of Afghanistan in the centre of the country, although the area is culturally and tribally linked to Kandahar Province in the south. The capital of Uruzgan is Tarinkot - Area: 12,640 km².

[25] Zabul – (Persian and Pashto: زابل) is a historic province in southern Afghanistan, in the heart of the historical region of Zabulistan. Zabul became an independent province from neighbouring Kandahar in 1963, with Qalat being named the provincial capital - Area: 17,343 km².

Anaconda the Pentagon requested the deployment of British Royal Marines, highly trained in mountain warfare. A number of missions were conducted over several weeks with varying results. The Taliban, who during the summer of 2002 numbered in the hundreds, avoided combat with U.S. forces and their Afghan allies as much as possible and melted away into the caves and tunnels of remote Afghan mountain ranges or across the border into Pakistan during these operations.

Whilst evading U.S. forces throughout the middle of 2002 the remnants of the Taliban gradually began to regain their confidence and began preparations to launch the insurgency that Mullah Muhammad Omar had promised during the Taliban's last days in power. During September Taliban forces began a recruitment drive in the Pashtun areas in both Afghanistan and Pakistan to launch a renewed jihad, or holy war, against the Afghan government and the U.S-led coalition. Pamphlets distributed in secret during the night also begun to appear in many villages in the former Taliban heartland in south-eastern Afghanistan calling for jihad. According to Afghan sources and a UN report Al Qaeda and Taliban fugitives established small mobile training camps along the border with Pakistan in order to train new recruits in guerrilla warfare and terrorist tactics. Most of the new recruits were drawn from the madrassas[26] or religious schools of the tribal areas of Pakistan from which the Taliban had originally arisen. Major bases, a few with as many as 200 men, were created in the mountainous tribal areas of Pakistan by the summer of 2003. The will of the Pakistani paramilitaries stationed at border crossings to prevent such infiltration was called into question, and Pakistani military operations proved of little use.

The Taliban gradually reorganized and reconstituted their forces over the winter, preparing for a summer offensive. They established a new mode of operation: gathered into groups of around 50 to launch attacks on isolated outposts and convoys of Afghan soldiers, police, or militia and then breaking up into groups of 5-10 men to evade

---

[26] madrasa - is the Arabic word for any type of educational institution, whether secular or religious.

subsequent offensives. U.S. forces in the strategy were attacked indirectly through rocket attacks on bases and improvised explosive devices. To coordinate the strategy Mullah Omar named a leadership council made up of ten men, which he was to lead, for the resistance. Five operational zones were created, assigned to various Taliban commanders such as the key Taliban leader Mullah Dadullah, in charge of Zabul province operations. Al Qaeda forces in the east had a bolder strategy of concentrating on the Americans by planning and executing elaborate and increasingly lethal ambushes.

The first sign that Taliban forces were regrouping came on 27 January 2003 during Operation Mongoose, when a band of fighters allied with the Taliban and Hezb-i-Islami were discovered and assaulted by U.S. forces at the Adi Ghar cave complex 24 km north of Spin Boldak. 18 rebels were reported killed, whilst no U.S. casualties were reported. The site was suspected of being a base for funnelling supplies and fighters from Pakistan. The first isolated attacks by relatively large bands of Taliban on Afghan targets also appeared around that time.

Throughout that summer attacks in the Taliban heartland increased in frequency. Dozens of Afghan government soldiers, NGOs and other humanitarian workers, and several U.S. soldiers died in raids, ambushes, and rocket attacks. In addition to these guerrilla attacks Taliban fighters began building up their forces in the district of Dai Chopan, a district in Zabul Province that also straddles Kandahar and Uruzgan and is at the epicentre of the Taliban heartland.

Dai Chopan district is a remote and sparsely populated corner of south-eastern Afghanistan composed of towering, Rocky Mountains interspersed with narrow gorges. Taliban fighters decided it would be the perfect area to make a stand against the Afghan government and the coalition forces. Over the course of the summer perhaps the largest concentration of Taliban militants gathered in the area since the fall of the regime, with up to 1,000 guerrilla fighters regrouping. Over 220 people, including several dozen Afghan police, were killed in August 2003 as Taliban fighters gained strength. As a result the coalition forces began preparing offensives to root out the rebel forces.

In late August 2005, Afghan government forces backed by U.S troops and heavy American aerial bombardment advanced upon Taliban positions within the mountain fortress. According to Afghan government estimated figures, after a battle lasting one week, Taliban forces were routed with up to 124 fighters killed. Taliban spokesmen denied the high casualty figure and U.S estimates proved to be somewhat lower.

From January 2006 a NATO International Security Assistance Force (ISAF) started to replace the U.S. troops of Operation Enduring Freedom in southern Afghanistan. The British 16th Air Assault Brigade, later reinforced by Royal Marines, formed the core of the force in Southern Afghanistan along with troops and helicopters from Australia, Canada and the Netherlands. The initial force consisted of roughly 3,300 British, 2,300 Canadian, 1,963 from the Netherlands, 290 from Denmark, 300 from Australia, and 150 from Estonia. The U.S. provided air support along with British, Dutch, Norwegian and French combat aircraft and helicopters.

At this time NATO's focus in southern Afghanistan was to form Provincial Reconstruction Teams with the British leading in Helmand Province. The Netherlands and Canada would lead similar deployments in Oruzgan Province and Kandahar Province respectively. Local Taliban figures voiced opposition to the incoming force and pledged to resist it. During 2006 Southern Afghanistan faced the deadliest spate of violence in the country since the ousting of the Taliban regime by U.S.-led forces in 2001 as the newly deployed NATO troops, led by British, Canadian and Dutch commanders battled resurgent militants.

Operation Mountain Thrust was launched on 17 May 2006 with the purpose of rooting out Taliban forces. In July Canadian Forces launched Operation Medusa supported by U.S., British, Dutch and Danish forces, in an attempt to clear the areas of Taliban fighters once and for all. Further NATO operations included the Battle of Panjwaii, Operation Mountain Fury and Operation Falcon Summit. NATO forces experienced intense fighting throughout the second half of 2006 and were successful in achieving tactical victories over the Taliban and denying areas to them - but the Taliban were not completely defeated and NATO had to continue operations into 2007.

In January and February 2007 British Royal Marines mounted Operation Volcano to clear insurgents from firing points in the village of Barikju, north of Kajaki. Operation Achilles followed this, a major offensive that started in March and ended in late May. The UK Ministry of Defence announced its intention to raise British troop levels in the country to 7,700 committed until 2009. Further operations such as Operation Silver and Operation Silicon were to keep up the pressure on the Taliban in the hopes of blunting their expected spring offensive.

On 4 March 2007 at least 12 civilians were killed and 33 injured by U.S. Marines in the Shinwar district of the Nangrahar[27] province of Afghanistan as the Americans reacted to a bomb ambush. The event has become known in the district as the Shinwar Massacre and was considered a propaganda coup for the Taliban. A Marine unit consisting of 120 men were found to be responsible for the attack. The entire unit was asked to leave the country because the incident had so damaged the unit's relations with the local Afghan population.

On 12 May 2007 ISAF forces killed Mullah Dadullah, the Taliban commander in charge of leading operations in the south of the country. Eleven other Taliban fighters were killed in the same firefight. This was a great success for the coalition, not only in terms of removing a major commander from the field, but also in terms of the propaganda it created. During the summer NATO forces achieved tactical victories over the Taliban at the Battle of Chora in Uruzgan Province, where Dutch and Australian ISAF forces are deployed. On 28 August 2007 at least 100 Taliban fighters and one Afghan National Army soldier were killed in several skirmishes in the Shah Wali Kot district of Kandahar province.

On 28 October 2007 around 80 Taliban fighters were killed in a 24-hour battle with forces from the U.S.-led coalition in Afghanistan's Helmand province. During the last days of October Canadian forces

---

[27] Nangarhar – one of the thirty-four provinces of Afghanistan in the east of the country. The capital city is Jalalabad. The population: 1,383,900, consisting of ethnic Pashtuns - area: 7,727 km².

surrounded around 300 militants near Arghandab and killed at least 50 of them. This was said to have stopped a potential Taliban offensive on Kandahar.

Taliban losses were mounting and yet it did not appear to blunt their effectiveness. The strength of Taliban forces was estimated by Western officials and analysts at about 10,000 fighters fielded at any given time, according to 30 October report in The New York Times, stating of that number only 2,000 to 3,000 are highly motivated, full-time insurgents. The rest are part-timers made up of alienated young Afghan men angry at bombing raids, or fighting in order to earn money.

In 2007 more foreign fighters were showing up in Afghanistan than ever before, according to Afghan and United States officials. An estimated 100 to 300 full-time combatants were foreigners, usually from Pakistan, Uzbekistan, Chechnya, various Arab countries, and perhaps even Turkey and western China. These had a tendency to be more fanatical and violent and often bring new skills such as the ability to post more sophisticated videos on the Internet as well as bomb-making expertise. The rising numbers of Coalition troops killed or wounded by roadside bombs did much to turn public opinion in Western countries, not least in the United Kingdom, against involvement in the war.

On 2 November 2007 Afghan security forces killed a top-ranking militant, Mawlawi Abdul Manan, after he was caught trying to cross into Afghanistan from neighbouring Pakistan. The Taliban confirmed his death. Eight days later on 10 November 2007 the Taliban ambushed a patrol in eastern Afghanistan killing six American and three Afghan soldiers while losing only one of their own insurgents. This attack brought the U.S. death toll to 100 for 2007 and making it the deadliest year for Americans in Afghanistan.

Security operations were conducted in the north by ISAF and Afghan forces including Operation Harekate Yolo I & II. Norwegian and German soldiers also took part in the operation. The exact death toll of insurgents killed in action was not disclosed at the time, but according to Norwegian news reports there were between 20 and 25 and the German Ministry of Defence verified a further 14. The operation ended on 6 November 2007.

The Battle of Musa Qala took place in December 2007. The principal fighting forces were the Afghan units, supported by British forces. Taliban forces were compelled to pull out of Musa Qala.

On 27 April 2008 President Karzai escaped another attempt on his life when gunmen opened fire during a military parade celebrating the nation's victory and liberation from the eight-year occupation of the Soviet Union. The fire-fight lasted about a quarter of an hour resulting in three dead and about a dozen wounded. On 29 April 2,300 U.S. Marines attacked the town of Garmsir in Helmand province a region of Afghanistan where the Taliban had a stronghold. In May Norwegian-led ISAF forces conducted a military operation in Badghis province.

It was at this time that the numbers of American combatants increased in number. In the first five months of 2008 the number of U.S. troops in Afghanistan increased by over 80 per cent with a surge of 21,643 more troops, bringing up the total number of U.S troops in Afghanistan from 26,607 in January to 48,250 in June.

On 13 June Taliban fighters demonstrated their ongoing strength, liberating all prisoners in Kandahar jail. This well-planned operation freed 1,200 prisoners, 400 of whom were Taliban prisoners-of-war, causing a major embarrassment for NATO in one of its operational centres in the country. In June the then British prime minster Gordon Brown announced the number of British troops serving in Afghanistan would increase to 8,030, a rise of 230 personnel.

13 July 2008 saw a coordinated Taliban attack launched on a remote NATO base at Wanat in the Kunar province. On 19 August French troops suffered their worse losses in Afghanistan in an ambush, and later in the month, an air strike targeted at a Taliban commander in Herat province killed 90 civilians.

Later that August began one of the largest operations by NATO forces in Helmand province Operation Eagle's Summit with the aim of bringing electricity to the region - they might not be able to win hearts and minds but they could ensure the people had electrical supplies.

On 3 September the war spilled over onto Pakistani territory for the first time when heavily armed commandos, believed to be US

Special Forces, landed by helicopter and attacked three houses in a village close to a known Taliban and Al Qaeda stronghold. The attack killed between seven and twenty people and according to local residents most of the dead were civilians. Pakistan responded furiously condemning the attack. The foreign ministry in Islamabad called the incursion a gross violation of Pakistan's territory.

On 6 September, in an apparent reaction to the recent cross-border attack, the federal government announced disconnection of supply lines to the allied forces stationed in Afghanistan through Pakistan for an indefinite period.

On 11 September militants killed two U.S. troops in the eastern part of the country. This brought the total number of U.S. losses to 113, making 2008 the deadliest year for American troops in Afghanistan since the start of the war. The year was also the deadliest for several European countries with soldiers fighting in Afghanistan. In September George Bush announced the withdrawal of over 8,000 troops from Iraq in the coming months and a further increase of up to 4,500 U.S. troops in Afghanistan.

An unnamed senior Pentagon official told the BBC that at some point between 12 July and 12 September 2008 President George W. Bush issued a classified order to authorize U.S. raids against militants in Pakistan. Pakistan said it would not allow foreign forces onto its territory and that it would vigorously protect its sovereignty. During September the Pakistan military stated that it had issued orders to open fire on American soldiers who crossed the Pakistan border in pursuit of militant forces.

On 25 September 25 Pakistani troops shot towards ISAF helicopters belonging to American troops. This caused confusion and anger in the Pentagon who asked for a full explanation into the incident. They denied that American helicopters were in Pakistani airspace. Pakistani President Asif Ali Zardari was quick to deny that shots were fired but instead insisted that the Pakistani troops shot flares to warn the Americans that they were in Pakistani airspace. This added to doubts expressed by certain Pentagon and Bush administration officials about the capabilities of the Pakistani Armed Forces to confront the militant threat. Tension mounted and added to the split, which occurred when American troops apparently landed on Pakistani soil to carry out an operation against militants in the North-West Frontier Province. Pakistan reacted angrily to the action saying 20 innocent villagers had been killed by U.S. troops.

On 1 October 2008 a suspected U.S. drone fired a missile against militants inside Pakistan's North-West Frontier Province near the Afghan border. It is believed that six people died in this incident. Such attacks, which did not cease, drew stiff response from Islamabad accusing the United States of violating their airspace; although Americans had expressed frustration at the lack or failure of action by the Pakistani side against the militants holed up on Pakistan soil.

The coalition forces were bringing 70 per cent of supplies through Pakistan every month, a total of 2,000 truckloads in all. During November and December 2008 there were multiple incidents of major theft, robbery, and arson attacks against NATO supply convoys in Pakistan. During an attack on 11 November 200 Taliban fighters in Peshawar hijacked a convoy carrying NATO supplies from Karachi to Afghanistan. The militants took two military Humvees[28] and paraded them in front of the media as trophies. Transport companies south of Kabul were reportedly paying protection money to the Taliban.

There were frequent attacks in the area east of the Khyber Pass in Pakistan, cargo trucks and Humvees set ablaze by Taliban militants. December 2008 saw half a dozen raids on depots with NATO supplies near Peshawar destroying 300 cargo trucks and Humvees. On 30 December 2008 Pakistani security forces shut down the supply line when they launched an offensive against Taliban militants who dominated the Khyber Pass region - after three days of fighting they declared the Khyber Pass open.

The Taliban destroyed an iron bridge on the highway between Peshawar and the Khyber Pass in February 2009. The other supply route through Pakistan via Chaman was briefly shut down in early 2009. On 10 January tribesmen used vehicles to block the road to protest against a raid by Pakistani counter-narcotics forces that left one villager dead. The protesters withdrew on 14 January after police

---

[28] humvee - a type of four-wheel-drive all-terrain military vehicle.

promised to take their complaints to the provincial authorities.

By January 2009 the Taliban was making the exaggerated claim that they had killed 5,220 foreign troops, downed 31 aircraft, destroyed 2,818 NATO and Afghan vehicles and killed 7,552 Afghan soldiers and police in 2008 alone. The Associated Press estimated that a total of 286 foreign military personnel were actually killed in Afghanistan in 2008.

The Khyber Border Coordination Centre between the U.S., Pakistan, and Afghanistan, at Torkham on the Afghan side of the Khyber Pass, had been in operation for nine months and had not been a success. Language barriers were a problem - it often comes as a surprise to both the Americans and British, that not all the world speaks their language fluently or at all. Border disputes between Pakistani and Afghan field officers did not help either, and long-standing mistrust among all three militaries had hampered progress.

In January about 3,000 U.S. soldiers from the 3rd Brigade Combat Team of the 10th Mountain Division moved into the provinces of Logar and Wardak. The troops were the first wave of an expected surge of reinforcements originally ordered by George W. Bush and increased by Barack Obama. In mid-February it was announced that 17,000 additional troops would be deployed to the country in two brigades and additional support troops - the 2nd Marine Expeditionary Brigade of about 3,500 from the 7,000 Marines, and the 5th Brigade, 2nd Infantry Division, a Stryker Brigade with about 4,000 of the 7,000 U.S. Army soldiers. The U.S. commander in Afghanistan General McKiernan had called for as many as 30,000 additional troops, effectively doubling the number of troops at that time in the country.

In response to the increased risk of sending supplies through Pakistan, work began on the establishment of a Northern Distribution Network (NDN) through Russia and several Central Asian republics. Initial permission for the U.S. military to move troop supplies through the region was given on 20 January 2009 after a visit by General Petraeus. Though U.S. forces were evicted from Manas Air Base in Kyrgyzstan only a few days later, on 3 February, transit agreements between the U.S. and Kyrgyzstan as well as the other

Central Asian republics remained in effect. The first shipment along the NDN route left on 20 February from Riga, Latvia, then travelled 3,212 miles (5,169 km) to the Uzbekistan town of Termez, on the Afghanistan border. U.S. commanders stated they hoped that 100 containers a day would be shipped along the NDN. By comparison 140 containers a day were being shipped through the Khyber Pass.

On 11 May 2009 Uzbekistan president Islam Karimov announced that the airport in Navoi, Uzbekistan was being used to transport non-lethal cargo into Afghanistan. Due to the still unsettled relationship between Uzbekistan and the United States following the 2005 Andijon massacre and subsequent expulsion of U.S. forces from Karshi-Khanabad airbase, U.S. forces were not involved in the shipment of supplies. Instead South Korea's Korean Air, which was at that time involved in overhauling Navois Airport, officially handled logistics at the site.

The concern of some analysts was that use of the NDN would come at the cost of increased Russian demands concerning missile defence and NATO enlargement. Additionally human rights advocates showed concerned that the U.S. was again working with the government of Uzbekistan who are often accused of violating human rights. Nevertheless, U.S. officials promised increased cooperation with Uzbekistan, including further assistance to turn the Navoi Airport into a major regional distribution centre for both military and civilian ventures.

Chapter 5

War Is Hell

In November 2006, the UN Security Council warned that Afghanistan may become a failed state because of increased Taliban violence, increasing illegal drug production, and fragile State institutions. Afghanistan was rated 10th on the failed states index, a rise from 11th in 2005. The central government had little power and control beyond the capital city of Kabul. From 2005 to 2006 the number of suicide attacks, direct fire attacks, and improvised explosive devices had all increased. Intelligence documents declassified in 2006 suggested that Al Qaeda, Taliban, Haqqani Network[29] and Hezb-i-Islami[30] sanctuaries had increased fourfold in Afghanistan. The campaign in Afghanistan successfully unseated the Taliban from power but was significantly less successful at achieving the primary policy goal of ensuring that Al Qaeda could no longer operate in Afghanistan.

The BBC News released an article on 19 June 2007 about life in

---

[29] Haqqani Network – considered the most ruthless branch of Afghan insurgency Group that started as part of anti-Soviet jihad - uses asymmetric warfare to fight against US-led NATO forces and the government of Afghanistan, and has moved into mafia-like violence, intimidation and extortion.

[30] Hezbi Islami (also Hezb-e Islami, Hezb-i-Islami, Hezbi-Islami, Hezb-e-Islami), meaning Islamic Party is an Islamist organization that was commonly known for fighting the Communist Government of Afghanistan and their close ally the Soviet Union. Founded and led by Gulbuddin Hekmatyar, it was established in Afghanistan in 1975. It grew out of the Muslim Youth organization, an Islamist organization founded in Kabul by students and teachers at Kabul University in 1969 to combat communism in Afghanistan. Its membership was drawn from ethnic Pashtuns, and its ideology from the Muslim Brotherhood and Abul Ala Maududi's Jamaat-e-Islami - Hezbi Islami seeks to emulate the Ikhwan militia of Saudi Arabia and to replace the various tribal factions of Afghanistan with one unified Islamic state. This puts them at odds with the more tribe-oriented Taliban.

Afghanistan since the U.S. occupation. The article focuses on the life of the villagers of Asad Khyl. What seems to have been suggested was that security in Afghanistan was better but poverty and corruption remained a major problem.

General David H. Petraeus, former head of U.S. troops in Iraq who was transferred to be head of their Central Command, admitted that the Taliban were gaining in strength. He cited the recent increase in attacks in Afghanistan and in neighbouring Pakistan. Petraeus also insisted that the challenges faced in Afghanistan were more complicated than the ones that were faced in Iraq during his tour of duty. He concluded that in order to turn around the situation the widespread militant sanctuaries and strongholds needed to be removed from inside Afghanistan.

On 1 October 2008 the top American General in Afghanistan, David McKiernan, warned that the situation in Afghanistan could get a lot worse. The international forces within Afghanistan have been unable to hold territory they have cleared because of the lack of troops. For this reason the general called for an extra three combat brigades (roughly 20,000 troops). Without this urgent rush of manpower the Taliban would be able to get back into the communities that were once cleared by international troops.

Generals always ask for more troops as if it were the solution to any problem; but this problem was also compounded by a lack of agreement on the objectives in the war, a lack of resources, lack of coordination, and too great a focus on the weak and corrupt central government at the expense of local and provincial governments. Indeed there was a developing appreciation that concentration needed to be on the region and not merely on Afghanistan. What American and NATO politicians and the Generals further admitted was that the war was not going to be a short one - decades were being mentioned. The Allies were digging in. In particular thousands of U.S. troops in Afghanistan stationed in large, permanent bases.

In February 2005 U.S. Senator John McCain (later to be the candidate for the American Presidency against Barack Obama in 2008) called for the establishment of permanent U.S. military bases in Afghanistan, saying such bases would be for the good of the American people because of the long-term security interests the U.S.

has in the region. McCain did not win the White House, but his view was generally accepted. He made the remarks while visiting Afghan President Hamid Karzai in Kabul as part of a five-member, bi-partisan Senate delegation travelling through the region for talks on security issues. The same delegation included the then Senator Hillary Clinton, later to become U.S. Secretary of State.

In mid-March 2005 U.S. Joint Chiefs of Staff Chairman General Richard Myers told reporters in Kabul that the U.S. Defence Department was studying the feasibility of such permanent military bases. At the end of March the U.S. military announced that it was spending $83 million on its two main air bases in Afghanistan, Bagram Air Base north of Kabul and Kandahar Air Field in the south of the country. A few weeks after this series of U.S. statements, in April 2005, during a surprise visit to Kabul by U.S. Defence Secretary Donald Rumsfeld, Afghan President Hamid Karzai hinted at a possible permanent U.S. military presence in Afghanistan, saying he had also discussed the matter with President Bush. Rumsfeld refused to be drawn on whether or not the U.S. wanted permanent American military bases in Afghanistan saying the final decision would come from the White House.

As of July 2008 hundreds of millions of dollars had been spent on permanent infrastructure for foreign military bases in Afghanistan, including a budget of $780 million to further develop the infrastructure at Kandahar Air Field base alone. Kandahar was described as a walled, multicultural military city that housed some 13,000 troops from 17 different countries - the kind of place where you can eat at a Dutch chain restaurant alongside soldiers from the Royal Netherlands Army. The Bagram Air Base run by the U.S. military was also expanding, with the U.S military buying land from Afghan locals in different places for further expansion of the base.

By January 2009 the U.S. had begun work on $1.6 billion worth of new permanent military installations. In February 2009 in London *The Times* newspaper repeated the story, stating that the United States intended to build new military bases in southern Afghanistan. One to be built in Kandahar province near the Helmand border, at Maiwand - a place famous as the site of the destruction of a British army during the Second Anglo-Afghan War - and another new U.S. military base to be built in Zabul, a province now largely controlled by the Taliban.

The Allies were in Afghanistan for the long haul. And not everyone was heartened by this dramatic build-up of an indefinite Western military presence. The government of Russia, strenuously seeking to regain its place at the top table of important nations, expressed disapproval. 'Is it all to fight a number of Taliban - 10,000, 12,000?' Zamir Kabulov, Russia's ambassador to Kabul questioned. 'Maybe this infrastructure, military infrastructure, [is] not only for internal purposes but for regional also?' This comment hit the nail on the head. Russia viewed the large and indefinite military build-up as a potential threat because (as once recognised by Sir Halford Mackinder[31]) Afghanistan's geographical location is a very strategic one, being close to the three main world basins of hydrocarbons: the Persian Gulf, Caspian Sea, and Central Asia. Other observers have also noted that through a stronger military presence in Afghanistan the U.S. may be seeking to strengthen its own position in the region to counter increasingly warm relations between India, Russia and China. And, of course, Afghanistan is a neighbour of Iran, still a main player in the region, as it has been ever since the time of Alexander the Great. The United States long ago entered the Great Game, the greatest game of all in the world, and, indeed, the only game of any significance. Except that to use the term 'game' is to diminish the stature of all who are risking their lives and their livelihoods every day.

The International Security Assistance Force[32] (ISAF) is an

---

[31] Sir Halford John Mackinder PC (15 February 1861 – 6 March 1947) was an English geographer, academic, and Director of the London School of Economics, who is regarded as one of the founding fathers of both geopolitics and geostrategy. In 1904 Mackinder gave a paper on '"The Geographical Pivot of History" at the Royal Geographical Society, in which he formulated the Heartland Theory. Whilst initially receiving little attention outside geography, this theory would later exercise some influence on the foreign policies of world powers.

[32] By mid 2009 ISAF numbers were: 58,390, of which more than 26,000 were Americans and eight and a half thousand British troops.

international stabilization force authorized by the United Nations Security Council on 20 December 2001. On 31 July 2006 the NATO-led International Security Assistance Force assumed command of the south of the country and by 5 October 2006 also of the eastern part of Afghanistan. Although most American's initially supported the initiative, the UN Security Council, and NATO, but many people throughout the world, Europeans in particular, soon began to oppose to the war. In a 47-nation June 2007 survey of global public opinion, there was considerable opposition to U.S. and NATO operations in Afghanistan. In only four out of the 47 countries surveyed was there a majority that favoured keeping foreign troops: the U.S. (50%), Israel (59%), Ghana (50%), and Kenya (60%). In 41 of the 47 countries, pluralities[33] wanted U.S. and NATO troops out of Afghanistan as soon as possible.

The opinions of the populace rarely count for much. Newspaper articles and television programmes sway people, and they generally know little, if anything, of the situation on the ground, and even less of the political and strategic issues involved. However, in fairness, it has to be said that since the June 2008 global survey, public opinion in Australia and Britain had also diverged from that in the U.S., and a majority of Australians and Britons wanted their troops to be brought home from Afghanistan. A September 2008 poll found that 56 per cent of Australians opposed the continuation of their country's military involvement in Afghanistan, while 42 per cent supported it. A November 2008 poll found that 68 per cent of Britons wanted their troops withdrawn within the ensuing 12 months. In the United States a September 2008 Pew survey found that 61 per cent of Americans wanted U.S. troops to stay until the situation has stabilized, while 33 per cent wanted them removed as soon as possible.

Public opinion at the beginning of the war also reflected this dichotomy between the United States and most other countries. When the invasion began in October 2001 polls indicated that about 88 per cent of Americans and about 65 per cent of Britons supported military action in Afghanistan. On the other hand, a large-scale 37-

---

[33] pluralities – (in the USA) the number of votes cast for a candidate who receives more than any other but does not receive an absolute majority.

nation poll of world opinion carried out by Gallup International in late September 2001 found that large majorities in most countries favoured a legal response, in the form of extradition and trial, over a military response to the events of 9/11. Only in 3 countries out of the 37 surveyed - the United States, Israel, and India - displayed majorities favouring military action in Afghanistan. In 34 out of the 37 countries surveyed the results found sizeable majorities that did not favour military action: in the United Kingdom (75%), France (67%), Switzerland (87%), Czech Republic (64%), Lithuania (83%), Panama (80%), Mexico (94%), and others. However, since the Taliban refused to hand over Osama bin Laden or his followers for trial, extradition was not a viable option by the time the war began. An Ipsos-Reid poll conducted between November and December 2001 showed that majorities in Canada (66%), France (60%), Germany (60%), Italy (58%), and the U.K. (65%) approved of U.S. air strikes while majorities in Argentina (77%), China (52%), South Korea (50%), Spain (52%), and Turkey (70%) opposed them. Polls are rarely valuable, and opinions tend to be based on emotional rather than rational responses.

The war has repeatedly been the subject of protests around the world starting with the large-scale demonstrations in the days leading up to the official launch of U.S. Operation Enduring Freedom under George W. Bush in October 2001 and every year since. Protesters consider the bombing and invasion of Afghanistan to be unjustified aggression. The death of thousands of Afghan civilians caused directly and indirectly by the U.S. and NATO bombing campaigns is also a major underlying focus of the protests. These people are often naïve liberals who will join any protest that affords shouting in the streets. There may well be legitimate concerns, and there are, but rent-a-crowd liberals know little of these.

Regarding civilian casualties of the War in Afghanistan from 2001 to the present day, there are no reliable figures and, given the nature of the conflict, there probably never will be. In time of war both or all sides commit atrocities - that is part of human nature when in extreme situations were individuals lose whatever moral compass they had in the first place. We need also to remember that individuals who would not normally commit an atrocity will often do so when they become part of a group, especially a group without proper central control, or with leaders who are prepared to countenance extreme behaviour. A mob or a herd is not merely a group of individuals – something else is added to the mix. One has only to observe the behaviour of people at football matches to understand that individuals within a herd do not act reasonably or responsibly.

The UN Assistance Mission in Afghanistan (UNAMA) has reported that in the year 2008 alone more than two thousand Afghan civilians were killed by armed conflict, this was the highest figure since the beginning of the invasion. Some have claimed that the figure is double this, and perhaps even higher than five thousand, but evidence is hard to obtain. While not all civilian casualties are inflicted by air strikes, it is probably correct to say that air strikes on villages and towns are responsible for high civilian death rates and casualties. There was a tacit admission of this when, in March 2009, General McChrystal announced new restrictions on air strikes in order to reduce civilian casualties. Whether this was to appease a restless electorate, it is impossible to know. What is certain is that air strikes continued but the emphasis from then onward appeared to be the hitting of insurgents in the border areas with Pakistan. In any case, in such a war as this, a fighter by night can become a peasant tilling his fields by day - a committed soldier will break ranks when it is time to return home to harvest the poppy seeds.

War is hell. Anyone who says different does not understand war. Yet a strange phenomenon appears to have developed in recent times, both in the USA and Britain, where a growing number of people have begun to think that wars can be conducted without civilian casualties. This goes even further with the belief that wars can be fought without military casualties. As soon as coffins started to be unloaded from transport planes, as witnessed on our television screens, there was a public demand in newspaper letters columns and on phone-in radio programmes, for the country to withdraw from the war. These people are at best naïve. One does not need to be a pacifist or a supporter of the conflict to know that in war there are certain to be casualties.

David Miliband, then Foreign Secretary in the UK government, in an article in the *Daily Telegraph* newspaper 17 August 2009, strongly defended the role of British troops in Afghanistan in the face of mounting criticism over the number of military casualties. The figure of military deaths had reached 204, 'a reminder of the bravery of our soldiers and the sacrifices they make every day. It was,' he said, 'understandable that people were asking questions: why the British were in Afghanistan, and for how long? People also wanted to know how long the conflict would continue and whether the loss of life was justified. The Coalition was in Afghanistan through necessity. As the home of international terrorism, the border region of Afghanistan and Pakistan remained the primary threat to Britain's national security. Having driven Al Qaeda out of Afghanistan, they must not be allowed to return under the safe umbrella of Taliban rule. British soldiers were fighting in a coalition of 42 allies and alongside Afghan government forces to push the Taliban out of the towns and villages and to ensure they stay out. One source of the Taliban's strength, but also its vulnerability, is that they are an amalgam of different groups – a coalition of convenience. They recruit foot soldiers at $10 a day. Narco-traffickers work with them to get safe passage for drugs. Warlords, believing the Taliban will win, position themselves for their own political advantage. Perhaps most crucially, Afghans, despite dreading the Taliban's return, fear that international forces will leave before the Afghan state is ready to protect them. So they hedge their bets. For many people - indeed for everyone - the name of the game is survival. Whether military breakthroughs are translated into strategic success depends on politics - crucially the ability of the political system to incorporate people currently acquiescent to or supportive of violence. International and Afghan forces can keep the insurgents on the back foot. But only legitimate, clean and competent Afghan government, recognising local tribal structures as well as national democratic ones, can provide an alternative focus for loyalty. Effective protection and a better life is the best way to keep the insurgency at bay. Yet a General Election roused little interest, and there was well-founded evidence of corruption, intimidation and vote rigging by the Karzai government in Kabul. This same Afghan government, deeply corrupt, must,' continued Miliband, 'deepen cooperation with its neighbours, particularly Pakistan. The Pakistani military offensive launched in April meant that for the first time the insurgency was being squeezed on both sides of the border.' Fine words from an intelligent politician intended for his own electorate. These words did not, however, state the truth of the situation - yet they did come close.

The mention of Pakistan is significant. The Coalition cannot afford to allow Pakistan to fall to the Taliban, Al Qaeda, the jihadists, the Islamist extremists - these names are almost interchangeable - because Pakistan is a nation with stocks of nuclear weapons. Al Qaeda with the bomb is a nightmare scenario, making the attack on the Twin Towers in New York, with the loss of three thousand civilian lives, look like a mild altercation at a tea party held at a local vicarage. Al Qaeda in possession of the Bomb has been described as Existential Horror.

It is not necessary to be a defender of the Taliban, certainly not, to accept that not everything done during the Taliban government in Afghanistan was unacceptable. In 2000 the Taliban issued a ban on opium production, which led to reductions in Pashtun Mafia opium production by as much as 90 per cent. Soon after the 2001 U.S. led invasion of Afghanistan opium production increased markedly. By 2005 Afghanistan had regained its position as the world's leading producer of opium, producing 90 per cent of the world's opium, most of which is processed into heroin and sold in Europe and Russia. While U.S. and allied efforts to combat the drug trade have been stepped up, the effort is hampered by the fact that many suspected drug traffickers are now leading officials in the Karzai government.

Recent estimates by the United Nations Office on Drugs and Crime (UNODC) estimate that 52 per cent of the nation's GDP, amounting to $2.7 billion annually, is generated by the drug trade. The rise in production has been linked to the deteriorating security situation, as production is markedly lower in areas with stable security. The poppy eradication policy propagated by the international community, and in particular the United States as part of their War on Drugs, has been a failure, exacerbated by the lack of alternative development projects to replace livelihoods lost as a result of poppy eradication.

Seeking to eradicate poppy cultivation, the Allies have succeeded only in increasing poverty in rural areas, not least in the south of Afghanistan. The extermination of the poppy crops is not seen as a viable option, due to the fact that the sale of poppies constitute the livelihood of Afghanistan's rural farmers. Opium is more profitable than wheat and destroying opium fields has lead to discontent and unrest amongst the population, and alternatives to poppy eradication have so far failed.

We hear a great deal these days about human rights. If truth is the first casualty of war, perhaps human rights are the second. This is not something that has arisen from the invasion in 2001. Afghanistan has suffered extensive human rights violations over the last twenty years. When armed factions struggle to achieve supremacy there is going to be abuses. War is not a game for gentlemen, and especially not civil conflict. The Taliban rose to power in 1998 and ruled Afghanistan for five years, during which time they became notorious for their human rights abuses against women.

According to Amnesty International[34] - a group that zealously seeks to find the truth in a situation and report it accurately, without fear, and without favour to any government or group - the Taliban commit war crimes by targeting civilians, including killing teachers, abducting aid workers and burning school buildings. Amnesty International claims that up to 756 civilians were killed in 2006 by bombs, mostly on roads or carried by suicide attackers belonging to the Taliban. In addition, Afghan warlords and political strongmen have been responsible for numerous human rights violations including kidnapping, rape, robbery, and extortion. This is certainly no land for the timid or the squeamish.

It has been claimed that top officials at the CIA authorized

---

[34] Amnesty International (AI) is a nonprofit, independent international organization that works zealously to protect Human Rights around the world. Founded in Britain in 1961 AI works to secure the release of people imprisoned for their beliefs, to ban the use of torture, and to abolish the death penalty.

controversial, harsh interrogation techniques. The Bush administration declared that Al Qaeda members captured on the battlefield were not subject to the Geneva Conventions as this was not a conventional war. Amnesty International stated in 2007 that an agreement to allow Canadian officials to visit enemy detainees in Afghanistan was aimed more at saving political face than keeping prisoners safe. Interrogation techniques included shaking and slapping, shackling prisoners in a standing position, keeping the prisoner in a cold cell and dousing them with water, and, most controversially of all water boarding.

Water boarding is a form of torture that consists of immobilizing the victim on his or her back with the head inclined backwards. Water is poured over the face and into the breathing passages. By forced suffocation and inhalation of water the subject experiences the sensation of drowning. Water boarding precipitates an almost immediate gag reflex. The technique does not inevitably cause lasting physical damage. It can, however, cause extreme pain, dry drowning, damage to lungs, brain damage from oxygen deprivation, and other physical injuries including broken bones due to struggling against restraints, lasting psychological damage or, if uninterrupted, death. This is not a new technique. The torturer's art is ancient, and has many variations. In 2007 it was reported that the CIA was using water boarding on extra-judicial prisoners and that the United States Department of Justice had authorized the boarding was sanctioned by the Bush administration. In January 2009, in one of the first acts of his presidency, Barack Obama banned the use of water boarding.

The Allies have alleged that the Taliban have used indefensible tactics too. It is alleged that Taliban uses civilians as human shields. NATO has pointed to the victims of air strikes in Farah[35] province in May 2009 in which the Afghan government claimed up to 150 civilians were killed. NATO stated that it had evidence that the

---

[35] Farah (Pashto/Persian: فراه) is one of the thirty-four provinces of Afghanistan, located in the western part of the country next to Iran. It is a spacious and sparsely populated province, divided into eleven districts and contains hundreds of villages. It has a population of about 925,016 that is multi-ethnic and mostly a rural tribal society.

Taliban forced civilians into buildings likely to be targeted by NATO aircraft involved in the battle. US Lieutenant Colonel Greg Julian, a spokesman for NATO's Afghanistan commander, said of the Taliban's tactics, 'this was a deliberate plan by the Taliban to create a civilian casualty crisis. These were not human shields; these were human sacrifices. We have intelligence that points to this. Patient after patient just kept telling the doctors their story and how they were forced by the Taliban to stay in these locations'.

There is little point in further cataloguing abuses by all parties in this conflict. War is hell, and it could be argued that in such a situation it is foolish to promulgate rules of conduct. The important thing is not to sling mud, to allege this and that, but to consider how the conflict may be terminated.

The First World War lasted four years, and World War II lasted six years, but The Afghanistan War has lasted far longer than both of these put together. During his short tenure as Allied commander in Afghanistan, American General Stanley McChrystal[36] asserted that troop deaths were a price worth paying. This was in response to criticisms, especially in NATO countries, that casualties were becoming too high, and that the invasion had proved unnecessary. McChrystal stated that, despite some progress being made, many indicators point to a general deterioration in the overall state of Afghanistan. If the government were to fall to the Taliban, he said, Afghanistan could again become a base for terrorism. 'We face not only a resilient and growing insurgency; there is also a crisis of confidence among Afghans - in both their government and the international community - that undermines our credibility and

---

[36] General Stanley McCrystal - in June 10, 2009 U.S. Senate gave approval for him to take command in Afghanistan, and he was promoted to General. Shortly afterward McChrystal assumed command of NATO operations. But his tenure was short and controversial. During a brief (less than 20 minutes) and hastily convened meeting at the White House with Obama on 23 June 2010, President Obama 'accepted' McChrystal's resignation. He was dubbed "The Runaway General" in an article written by freelance journalist Michael Hastings in *Rolling Stone* magazine, July 8–22, 2010 issue.

emboldens the insurgents'.

General McChrystal's suggested remedy was an increase in resources, both military and civilian. He said that he needed a 'jump' in resources, both civilian and military to defeat the insurgency. Additional resources alone would not win the war, but under-resourcing, as he put it, could lose the war. In addition, McChrystal said a new strategy was needed. It was vital to win the support of the Afghan population. This is another way of saying that the Allies must win the hearts and minds of the people being invaded and not likely to be successful. The Allies are foreign troops and, as memories of Taliban puritanism fade, it is likely that many Afghans will choose their own people over foreigners. Those that do not revert to support for the Taliban are likely to side with the many warlords. 'Additional resources are required', said the General, 'but focusing on force or resource requirements misses the point entirely. The key take away from this assessment is the urgent need for a significant change to our strategy and the way that we think and operate'. The war, he stated - and this view has been echoed by British generals - is going to take decades rather than years. It is important to convince the Afghan people that there is a resolve to win the war against the Taliban, and they need not fear given their support. General McChrystal also referred to the size of the Afghan national army. As he spoke its strength was about 92,000 men. It needs to be increased to 240,000. The police force needed to grow from 84,000 police to 160,000. Also, possibly as a nod to liberal opinion in the United States and in NATO countries, McChrystal said that all detention centres, including the prison at Bagram Air Base, were to be eventually handed over to the Afghan authorities when they have the capacity to run them. If he believed that this would improve the situation in prisons in Afghanistan he was deluding himself.

Chapter 6

Can The West Win The War In Afghanistan?

If the history of foreign invasions into Afghanistan is anything to go by, the answer to the question can the West win the war in Afghanistan must be in the negative. The British at their height of power in Victorian times could not hold the country, and in more recent times the Soviets suffered a crushing defeat after a decade of wasted armour and manpower. Now the Americans have joined the Great Game, which is not a game at all, but a deadly and brutal series of battles, renewed strategies, troop surges - and for what? This is the question that is being asked everywhere in the West.

So why are we in Afghanistan? Why are lives being lost? When will withdrawal begin?[37] Promises are in hand for a series of withdrawals by the end of 2014, but many think tanks doubt that because the U.S. wants a permanent base there to police that region. What many people do not ask, or dare not ask, what would be the result if the West were to withdraw? It is said that history repeats itself, if that is true will the U.S. abandon Afghanistan as they did after the withdrawal of the Red Army? After what seemed an easy initial victory, and it was relatively easy, the Taliban is again resurgent. Now the West appears to be repeating all the mistakes made by the Soviets. The Soviet hierarchy believed that they could use a small number of Marxists to create a compliant satellite in the very heartland. They were wrong. With American assistance to the Mujahedeen there was strong resistance to the invader. Afghanistan is a Muslim country, and Islam has not accepted the tenets of Marxism, especially one imposed by a foreign army. The Soviets had to withdraw, and inside Russia there was popular support for the withdrawal, and likewise in the U.S. today.

When the U.S. defeated the Taliban it needed only three hundred American Special Forces to assist the Afghans. Then the Americans

---

[37] At the time of writing these were the questions on everybody's minds, and President Obama's promise of large-scale withdrawal of troops on the ground had not yet begun.

started to make some of the mistakes made earlier by the Soviets. There was initial goodwill in many parts of Afghanistan. People were pleased to see the back of the repressive Taliban regime. What, perhaps, was needed - and this is the opinion of some critics - was to build up the government and economic structures of the country and then get out swiftly; but instead of such a strategy, the U.S. seems bent on the imposition of a modern democratic country. Democracy is as alien to the vast majority of Afghans as is Marxism, so by duplicating the errors of the Soviets, will they also perhaps pay the same price in terms of ill will, loss of material, and loss of lives. We cannot try to create a modern, centralized, democratic state in Afghanistan from the top down using foreign troops - from fifty countries remember – in order to impose a Western-style democracy.

By Western standards elections are fraudulent and ridden with corruption. For many people Hamid Karzai, titular President of his country, is little more than the Mayor of Kabul. American intelligence sources have admitted, in muted voice perhaps, that Karzai's government is corrupt and that large swathes of territory are once again falling under Taliban control. In part the resurgence of the Taliban has been due to its cowing of the people, but there is also the view, recognised throughout the ages, that people will support their own kind against foreigners, no matter what the good intentions of those foreigners might be.

U.S. Instruments To Contain China

To prevent the rise of China as the regional hegemon, The U.S. has pursued three courses of action involving Rare Earth Metals, pipelines, and alliances.

1. China has the world's largest reserve of rare metals and controls 97% of the worlds supply. If preliminary estimates are correct Afghanistan has the world's sixth largest reserves of these metals. By Washington effectively controlling this alternative source, the U.S. and the rest of the industrialised world would be less dependent on China. It would strengthen the geopolitical position of Washington whilst simultaneously weakening that of Beijing.

2. China's growing economy needs access to the oil and gas reserves of Central Asia, which requires unfettered use of the oil and gas

pipelines. Dr Brzezinski advocated the U.S. geopolitical objective in central Asia be the control of these pipelines, "Thus, at stake in this conundrum are geopolitical power, [and] access to potentially great wealth…Until the collapse of the Soviet union, access to the region was monopolised by Moscow. All rail transport, gas and oil pipelines, and even air travel were channeled through the center. Russian geo-politicians would prefer it to remain so since they know that whoever either controls or dominates access to the region is the one most likely to win the geo-political and economic prize." The prize is Eurasia. As Dr Brzezinski noted, "The momentum of Asia's economic development is already generating massive pressures for the exploration and exploitation of new sources of energy and the Central Asian region and the Caspian Sea basin are known to contain reserves of natural gas and oil that dwarf those of Kuwait, the Gulf of Mexico, or the North Sea." Limit China's access to those reserves and pipelines and China's economic growth is restricted. If China's economic growth is restricted, Beijing lacks the financing to modernise and expand her military capabilities. Without increased economic and military power, China lacks the ability to project political influence. It is, thereby, prevented from emerging as a regional hegemon.

3. To limit China's growing political influence and economic power in the region, the U.S. promotes alliances having a dual purpose of containment and balance of power. The containment strategy consists of a series of 'alliances' between the U.S. and countries bordering China stretching in a southern arc from Northeast Asia to Southeast Asia to South Asia to Central Asia. Building on existing Cold War treaties between the U.S. and its traditional allies Japan, South Korea, and Taiwan, Washington has expanded this alliance to include Afghanistan and former adversary Vietnam. Based on shared concerns over Chinese power and intentions the U.S. seeks to include in this 'coalition' Laos, Cambodia, Thailand, Malaysia, India, Kazakhstan, Uzbekistan, and Kyrgyzstan. The balance of power strategy rests on supporting India a multi-party democracy pursuing free market economies, as the alternative model to China for Asia's economic development. Only India has the territorial and population size and economic potential to be China's rival. It is assumed there

will be a natural evolution in Indian foreign policy, as the country's economy grows so will its political aspirations, fuelled by ongoing friction in Indian-Chinese relations over border disputes, China's support of Pakistan, and India's 'support' of the Dalai Lama and the Tibetan government in exile.

An Evaluation of U.S. Policy in Both Short-term and Long-term

In the short term, U.S. policies seeking to prevent China from becoming a regional hegemon has not been successful. China is not a hegemon, but its economic power and influence continues to grow and the potential for China emerging as one still exists.

In the long term, however, this U.S. objective may be realised, not by the success of current policy, but from the unintended consequences of China's new economy. China's economic strength is impressive. It has emerged as the world's second largest economy after the U.S. One of the fastest-growing economies over the last three decades China averaged an annual growth rate of 10%. It is now the world's largest exporter and the world's second largest importer. The engine driving this economic growth, however, has largely been just one region, China's southern coast. The consequences of this pose a danger not just to China's future economic stability, but to its continued territorial integrity. Growing economic disparity between coast and interior can ignite social unrest. An estimated 250 million migrant workers and their dependents from the interior have flooded the rich coastal cities. Of a labour force estimated at 800 million roughly half are employed in state owned enterprises. Many of the state owned enterprises are non-productive. If Beijing does not phase out government subsidies to such industries there will be an economic crisis. If Beijing does phase out subsidies and even a fraction of those 300 to 400 million workers become unemployed, China may erupt in a social revolution.

The objective of Beijing is to prevent such social and economic problems from aggravating the ethnic minorities' issue. Officially there are 55 ethnic minorities in China including Hui, Manchus, Mongols, Tibetans, Uyghurs and Zhuangs. They constitute 8% of the total population, but occupy 60% of the territory. The existential threat to the Chinese state posed by the ethnic minorities' issue, however, resides within the ethnic "Chinese" majority.

China's fear is replicating the fall of the Soviet Union. When it's borderlands, Central Asia and Transcaucasus were lost, the Russian core shattered into three states: Byelorussia, Ukraine and Russia. If China should lose its borderlands, Tibet and Xinjiang, the Chinese core may similarly shatter.

The Chinese core consists of Han or ethnic Chinese. It constitutes approximately 92% of the country's population and numbers one 1.2 billion - but the term is an artificial concept since it incorporates two distinct geographic, historic, and ethno-linguistic communities, North and South "Chinese". Of the 1.2 billion Han, over 300 million, nearly a third of the total, are South "Chinese". While their region drives China's economy they speak eight languages, mutually unintelligible to the Mandarin language spoken by the north. In the past these ethno-linguistic differences, which are reinforced by geographic boundaries have led to the emergence of separate northern and southern states. This occurred in the 3rd, 4th, 5th 6th, 10th and 12th centuries. Just because it has not reoccurred in eight centuries does not preclude the possibility of it re-occurring in the future, as the fate of Russia with the fall of the Soviet Union demonstrated.

Should economic downturn and social unrest weakened the grip of China's Communist Party and the state fragments, South China has the necessary economic, physical, and demographic resources to become a viable independent country like Ukraine. Neither South China nor North China would possess the ability to become a regional hegemon and the U.S. geopolitical objective of preventing China from being able to dominate Eurasia would be accomplished.

Chapter 7

What about Pakistan?

What about Pakistan indeed! This is the great conundrum. There are no easy answers. Certainly I have none to offer.

Afghanistan has ancient links with Pakistan because of its geographical contiguity and traditional, cultural and linguistic connections. Any development in Afghanistan since 1947 has had direct implications on Pakistani society for one reason or another. Following the Soviet defeat the unstable situation in Afghanistan ensured that it became a secure harbour for terrorists and extremists from several parts of the world and not merely from within the sub-continental region. Pakistan has subsequently suffered a great deal. The recent American invasion, the war against terrorism, insurgencies and uprisings in the Federally Administered Tribal Areas (FATA)[38] of Pakistan is solid and substantial evidence of instability within

---

[38] The Federally Administered Tribal Areas (FATA) - (Pashto: وسطي اپښتونخوا منځنی سیمی، قبایلي) is a semi-autonomous tribal region in northwestern Pakistan, bordering Pakistan's provinces of Khyber Pakhtunkhwa and Balochistan to the east and south, and Afghanistan's provinces of Kunar, Nangarhar, Paktia, Khost and Paktika to the west and north. The Federally Administered Tribal Areas comprise seven tribal agencies (districts) and six frontier regions, and are directly governed by Pakistan's federal government through a special set of laws called the Frontier Crimes Regulations (FCR). The region was annexed in the 19th century during the British colonial period, and though the British never succeeded in completely calming unrest in the region, it afforded them some protection from Afghanistan. The territory is almost exclusively inhabited by the Pashtuns, who also live in the neighbouring Khyber Pakhtunkhwa and Afghanistan and are Muslim by faith. Main towns of the territory are Parachinar, Miranshah, Razmak, Kaniguram, Wana, Kalaya, Landi Kotal, Ghalanai and Khaar. Total population was estimated in 2000 to be about 3,341,070 people, or roughly 2% of Pakistan's population. Only 3.1% of the population resides in established townships. It is thus the most rural administrative unit in Pakistan.

Afghanistan.

Secondly the ever-increasing role of India in the region has posed serious threats to the security of Pakistan as well as Afghanistan and the government and people of Pakistan and Afghanistan need to explore ways, and in fact are taking action, to try and safeguard their vital interest in the region. Questions like why is India throwing so much money into Afghanistan and increasing troop activity along its borders? Why is India funding more than a dozen consulates inside destabilised Afghanistan? These types of questions spark many doubts into people's minds and they must be answered before the sparks become flames, which can simmer and burn.

Reliable intelligence points to the fact that the Taliban and others operate out of Pakistan. The nature of the uncharted border makes this almost inevitable, and in modern times it has become accepted by most countries that if your enemy is attacking you from outside, then you have the right to instigate cross-border reprisals. It would also appear that Al Qaeda is no longer operating from inside Afghanistan. Osama bin Laden was found inside Pakistan and is now dead, and rumours persist that his loyal supporters continue to operate from inside the country.

So the Allies attack what they believe to be terrorist units on Pakistani soil, often using drone[39] aircraft. Again questions arise - can these drone attacks solve the issue? Surely the answer is emphatically no. The use of drone attacks is doing far more harm than healing wounds. Poor innocent women and children are dying every day and leaving behind grieving family members who become prime targets for those who would recruit and cultivate terrorists. Therefore the consequences of such attacks on the innocent civilian population are creating more terrorists than ever before.

Drones are remotely operated. They are not missiles: they can be

---

[39] drone or unmanned aerial vehicle (UAV) - an aircraft without a human pilot on board. Flight is controlled either autonomously by computers in the vehicle, or under the remote control of a pilot on the ground or from inside another vehicle. Uses aerodynamic forces to provide vehicle lift, can be expendable or recoverable and can carry a lethal or nonlethal payload.

directed, retrieved, and used again and again. They are usually powered by jet engines. They are useful for sending to remote areas, with a pre-programmed plan and a specific target. As well as attack missions, drones are also used for aerial reconnaissance.

There has been Allied success in using drones to target and kill known Al Qaeda and other militant leaders seeking sanctuary in Pakistan. A missile fired by a U.S. drone killed top Al Qaeda operations chief and two other militant commanders in the volatile North Waziristan region of Pakistan in September 2009. Ilyas Kashmiri was a native Pakistani. Pakistani military and intelligence sources said Kashmiri was killed on 7 September in the Machikhel area of North Waziristan. Two other local militant commanders, Hanifullah Janikhel and Kaleemullah, were also killed.

In August 2009 a drone strike in South Waziristan killed Pakistani Taliban leader Baitullah Mehsud, the most-wanted militant in the country, accused of engineering suicide bombings of civilian and military targets. U.S. drone strikes have killed several other prominent Al Qaeda militants in recent years including Abu Hamza Rabia, an Egyptian suspected of heading Al Qaeda's international operations, senior Al Qaeda leader Abu Laith al Libi, and Abu Sulayman Jazairi, an Algerian explosives specialist.

Although the United States' tactic of using drones to attack Al Qaeda and Taliban militants in Pakistan's tribal areas has been quite successful, of its other operations it has also been the source of public discord between the Pakistani government and Washington. Although Pakistani leaders publicly condemn the attacks because of the civilian casualties they sometimes cause, it is widely believed that they tacitly allow the strikes. In the case of Mehsud's death, Pakistani intelligence helped the U.S. pinpoint his location within Waziristan. Also the Pakistan army has directly confronted militants on home soil on numerous occasions. One such was the capture in the Swat valley of Sher Mohammed Qasab, a Taliban commander. Qasab was arrested in the Charbagh area of the valley that militants controlled before the Pakistani military launched a major offensive to drive them out in late April 2009. Qasab has been accused of personally beheading captured Pakistan soldiers, and also of setting fire to a girls' school in Swat. The military announced he was captured after he and his sons exchanged gunfire with troops - three of his sons were killed and a fourth was captured.

Pakistan in many respects is an unstable country. It has in its short history been beset by several military coups and failed coup attempts. Civilian governments have usually been short-lived, ineffective, and corrupt. Since independence in 1947, Pakistan has fought three wars against India, lost East Pakistan (now the independent state of Bangladesh) and had the long-running dispute of the Kashmir region. Despite there being a 95 per cent Muslim population, in Kashmir Pakistani soldiers police a fragile border, and strive to avoid, or at least dampen down sparks that may at any time produce a fresh conflagration with India.

In a country potentially riven with provincial and tribal differences, there is only one group within society that cuts across these deep-seated differences, and that is the military. It is not surprising that the periods of greatest stability and progress have been when a military dictator such as Ayub Khan, Zia ul Haq or Pervez Musharaff has been at the helm of government. The army cuts across tribal divisions; it has the power to mobilise quickly, and suppress discord; moreover, it is the one force that many Pakistanis trust. The Army has been the target after they started large-scale military operation against Taliban operating within Pakistan and supported from across the border. There is clear evidences that RAW (Indian Intelligence Agency) which has strong ties with the Northern Alliance government in Afghanistan is spending millions of dollars to bolster insurgency within Pakistan.

The Pakistan military has taken punitive action against Taliban militants by launching massive air strikes against its border region strongholds in retaliation for the Peshawar School massacre that left 132 children and nine staff dead in one of the worst terrorist incidents in the country's history. In an attack that provoked horror and fierce international condemnation, seven members of Tehrik-e-Taliban, Pakistan dressed in army uniform and wearing suicide vests, stormed the Army Public School in the early morning on Tuesday 16 December 2014 and began their shooting spree. Fire fights with Pakistan Special Forces continued for about eight hours before the school was cleared. Pakistani security forces said commandos killed some of the attackers and others had blown themselves up. Tehrik-e-Taliban claimed responsibility for the attack, saying it was in revenge for a ferocious army offensive named Zerb-e-Azb that has been underway in tribal areas since the summer and left an estimated 1,000 militants dead and tens of thousands of people displaced.

These brutal killings at the army school at Peshawar are one glaring example of outside agencies bolstering insurgency inside Pakistan. After the Peshawar incident during internal operations the Law Enforcement Agencies (LEAs) apprehended a few foreigners operating nexuses within Pakistan. The discovery of such kinds of activities is quite alarming. I strongly believe planned disruption of this nature creates more panic in the society and is not good for the country or the region as a whole.

The wrong distribution of power in Afghanistan has created a divide within society. The current power-sharing formula is not working. Some Western observers have concluded that, because of this, what Afghanistan needs is a strong man in Kabul, a military dictator. This may well be true. But if such a dictator were installed by the United States, he would surely be ineffective. He would be seen, and rightly so, as a stooge of the invading foreigners. Neither was Karzai the right man. Such a leader would have to come from within. Perhaps even now there is a young colonel in the nascent Afghan army who will one day seize control. Yet, could such a man command support, and establish control in a country so divided by tribe, by loyalty to warlords, and when half the population has fled into exile? And would the United States government, wedded to its notions of democracy, allow such a leader to emerge and take control?

The conflict and instability in Afghanistan in the aftermath of 9/11 attacks and their regional implications had very negative repercussions for the years following the US invasion of Afghanistan not only saw a huge influx of Afghan refugees across the border into Pakistan but also witnessed a sudden spike in the frequency and scale of terrorist attacks in Pakistan. The cumulative impact of these developments adversely impacted the overall growth rate in all major sectors of the economy. Pakistan continues to pay a heavy price both in the economic and security terms due to this situation and a substantial portion of precious national resources both men and material, have been diverted to address the emerging security challenges for the last several years. The rise of violent extremism and an increase in terrorism in Pakistan due to instability in Afghanistan not only caused serious damage to Pakistan's economy but has also been responsible for widespread human suffering due to indiscriminate attacks against the civilian population.

Afghanistan has suffered from wars that have happened from time to time, but its neighbouring countries, including Pakistan, have also suffered. After the Russian invasion of Afghanistan in 1979, more than 3 million Afghan refugees sought shelter in Pakistan. Russia lost almost 15,000 soldiers and many wounded. In 1988 the United States, Pakistan, Afghanistan, and the Soviet Union signed an agreement by which Russia would withdraw its troops and this was completed in 1989. After the Russian invasion a group of tribal and urban groups arose and all of these known collectively as the mujahidin, who afterwards formed into the Taliban. Even after the end of this Russian invasion the Afghan refugees have stayed in Pakistan and created an extra burden on the economy of the country. As with all desperate immigrants they provide cheap labour, which creates unemployment to local workers. Most of the Afghan immigrants have no documentation of any kind. Hardly any of them have ID or any record to their permanent location, this has offered some of the culprits an edge because they are not afraid to be identified. Most of the drug dealers, illegal arms dealers, car thieves, and smugglers are Afghan refugees who have made their permanent shops within the borders areas. Easy access to illegal weaponry, even to common people at a very reasonable price, has promoted the Kalacov Culture - 9 mm pistol easily procured at the low price of only Rs 3600, $45 and made in Dara Adam Khail in Pakistan. The Pakistan Army is continually involved in clearing such illegal activity.

Pakistan's support to fight against terrorism has not been reciprocated by the U.S. government in the same spirit and sincerity as is shown by Pakistan. The accelerated growth in Pakistan is not due only to U.S. financial support or facilitation. Pakistan as a nuclear power is too precious for the entire world. The developed world would not like Pakistan to crumble as it would create chaos and might land the nuclear arsenal in the wrong hands. Their support in the war against terror to the U.S. has in fact proved to be counterproductive for Pakistan's economy. As a front line state against war on terrorism Pakistan is subjected to many restrictions.

For the actual promotion and development of Pakistan's economy the following policy options are compulsory, as Pakistan needs trade not only aid.
1. U.S. should give market access to Pakistan especially for its textile sector.
2. Transfer of technology is required that will provide Pakistan a base for competition in the region.
3. Joint economic ventures should be made. These will be helpful to create Pakistan-US long-term bilateral relationship and will remove the image of Pakistan as a client state.
4. Visa restrictions should be eased for Pakistani businessmen and exporters.
5. Two thirds of U.S aid should be reserved for the development of economic programmes and one-third to security assistance.
6. Consistency in economic policies should be ensured through stable political government.
7. Civil and political institutions should be strengthened; their strength will ensure economic stability.

The main concern, in my opinion, is that if this blame game between Afghanistan, Pakistan and USA continues then we will not see peace in the region, and a destabilized Afghanistan and Pakistan is in no one's best interest and for obvious reasons.

Chapter 8

Strategy Debate Confusion

British and American generals have been calling for more troops to be sent to Afghanistan in the recent past, as if a surge were the answer. It might be a short-term solution in that areas of land might well be reclaimed from Taliban control, but it would be short-lived. In the same way politicians talk glibly of winning the hearts and minds of Afghans within the country. This is nonsense. Foreign invaders may be welcome to begin with, bringing order out of chaos, perhaps, but they soon outstay their initial welcome. Any chance of winning hearts and minds was lost within weeks of the invasion.

Speaking in London, the American army General Stanley A. McChrystal said he opposed strategies that would require fewer troops and focus on fighting Al Qaeda and the Taliban leadership through drone attacks, air strikes and similar approaches. Some Obama administration officials, including Vice President Joe Biden, favour such an approach with view to reducing casualties. However, counterinsurgency advocates have said that a narrow war effort would leave the Afghan government unprotected from encroachment by the Taliban or other extremist organizations.

It is this strategy debate that is at the heart of a sweeping review requested by President Obama as the administration grapples with a tainted Afghan presidential election, escalating violence and mounting allied casualties. General McChrystal was a participant at a meeting in Washington. He said: 'A strategy that does not leave Afghanistan in a stable position is probably a short-sighted strategy'. The general's repeated requests for more troops on the ground have been refused, at least until a new broader strategy has been agreed. In his speech to the London-based policy group, McChrystal did not make an explicit plea for more troops, but said that the White House debate was over the goals and objectives of the Afghanistan mission.

General McChrystal spoke again in London as the U.S. Senate debated a proposal to demand he testify about the war before lawmakers. Senator John McCain, who lost the presidential contest to

President Obama, was among those who wanted McChrystal to testify. McChrystal did not testify in open Congressional forum but he has repeated his view that the U.S. and its allies have not provided enough resources for the operations in Afghanistan, blaming the shortfall for a 'serious and deteriorating' situation. The fight, he said, must be redefined. 'The objective is the will of the Afghan people'. The war, McChrystal said, was ultimately political. All wars are. 'At the end of the day, we don't win by destroying the Taliban, we don't win by body counts, we don't win by number of successful military raids or attack', he said. 'We win when the people decide we win'.

The truth is that there are now generals and politicians on the Allied side who are ready to admit that the war in Afghanistan could possibly be lost. It has long been known that the war could not be won but the admission that defeat is possible is a new response, and one that deserves to be given a serious attention. That is why; surely, the inclusion of elements of the Taliban in a national government for Afghanistan is being talked about.

So why not, asks another group of vocal critics, get out of Afghanistan and save the lives of our soldiers, and allow the Afghans to stew in their own divisive juices; even if that means the return to Kabul of a Taliban government; even if it means brutal reprisals, the settling of scores on a large scale? It would not be the first bloodbath in history but it would be an important one for the twenty-first century. Having been fed many lies by a discredited government - weapons of mass destruction, immigration numbers, education standards, the Lisbon Treaty, boom and bust - the people of the United Kingdom are surely in no mood to trust their government. Pictures of coffins draped in the Union flag arriving back in England has led to people questioning the reasons for involvement in Afghanistan, and questioning the cost of British lives. There are similar stirrings in the United States and, to a lesser extent, in NATO countries. No matter how many times Gordon Brown and subsequently David Cameron tell the British people that soldiers are dying in Helmand to make safe the streets of London, polls keep showing that a majority rejects his assertion.

Ever since 2006, when John Reid, then Secretary for Defence, offered hope that British troops could be home within three years - an outcome that seemed unlikely even then - the government has been on the wrong side of public opinion. With more than 300 fatalities, and scores injured, the price of engagement is one the British voters are reluctant to pay. There is less stomach for a fight, and the left - for it is mainly the left - is mobilising this discontent to mount a campaign for disengagement. If the United Kingdom were to disengage, Germany and other NATO countries would not be far behind, and perhaps American political strategy would be in ruins.

The Anti-War Party is not a party in the political sense: it is a coalition of pacifists, peaceniks, leftists, those who are always ready to beat the USA with a big stick, and those who look at the situation in Afghanistan and become defeatist. Those of us whilst not belonging to the Anti-War coalition nevertheless perceive the notion that the Allies will be able, after a bloody military campaign, to leave behind a 'normalised', democratic Afghanistan, free from the Taliban, free from the influence of Al Qaeda, and with sufficient resources and appetite to police itself; but this idea tests credulity beyond all sensible bounds. Even if it were not corrupt the Karzai administration in Kabul would by itself never be able to contain the Taliban. General Sir David Richards, ex head of the British army, admitted as much when he said in August 2009 that the British could be involved in Afghanistan for another thirty to forty years.

Whether or not the Allies remain in Afghanistan, fighting an asymmetric war that neither side can win in the field, the war will continue. It will, perhaps, be fought in the streets of Paris, of London, of Jakarta, of Mumbai. With a global conflict looming, the calls of the Anti-War coalition to quit Afghanistan are almost irrelevant. What is certain, is that Pakistan will be involved - indeed, is heavily involved even as I write — and that the outcome of Pakistan's involvement will in many ways be crucial to the outcomes.

So what has been the relationship between Pakistan and Taliban, and why are so many Taliban fighters within Pakistan itself, not least in the Federally Administered Tribal Areas? With the withdrawal of the Soviets in 1989 the heroes of the moment were the Mujahedeen who had, with covert American assistance, done so much to harry the Russian invaders. But the popularity of the Afghan Mujahedeen decreased with the passage of time. Gangs roamed the countryside looting shops and committing other crimes. The area most affected was Kandahar, where the people sought relief from heroes who had in effect become bandits. The answer appeared to lie with a new force called the Taliban.

The world first became aware of the Taliban in 1994 when they were appointed by Islamabad to protect a convoy trying to open up a trade route between Pakistan and Central Asia. The group comprised of Afghans trained, along with former Mujahedeen, in religious schools in Pakistan. Later they captured Kandahar beginning a remarkable advance that led to the capture of the capital, Kabul, in September 1996.

The aims and objectives of the Taliban were made clear - the restoration of peace in Afghanistan; disarming the local population; implementing Sharia law. In an interview with the BBC, General Pervez Musharraf claimed that 'our national security compulsions as far as Afghanistan is concerned are, that the Pashtuns of Afghanistan have to be on Pakistan's side'. Pakistan's backing for the Taliban was explained in different ways. Some commentators saw it as Pakistan's relentless search for 'strategic depth' in the event of conventional war between India and Pakistan, while others pointed out that there were profits to be made from oil and gas pipelines from central to south Asia through a stable Afghanistan.

Circumstances change and, in politics as in wars, yesterday's enemy can become today's friend. The presence of the Taliban in Pakistan became a matter of contention between Islamabad and the Americans and their allies. The Allies claimed the right to cross borders in pursuit of the Taliban, but Pakistan countered by saying that its territorial integrity should not be compromised.

Following the US-led invasion of Afghanistan in 2001, Taliban and Al Qaeda fighters fled into Pakistan's tribal area, especially to Waziristan, spawning a Pakistani Taliban movement. Baitullah Mehsud was formally anointed head of the Taliban Movement of Pakistan in late 2007, although there remain Taliban groups that are not in his network.

By the middle of 2009, under pressure from the United States and, concerned at terrorist attacks in its own cities, the Pakistan government, now led by Asif Ali Zardari, widower of Benazir Bhutto, with Yousaf Raza Gilani for the first four years and then Raja Pervaiz Ashraf as his prime minister, decided to tackle the problems occasioned by the presence in the country of a large armed contingent that did not owe allegiance to Islamabad. The offensive risked engulfing the country in bloodshed as Baitullah Mehsud's terrorist network spans Pakistan, but the move seemed to finally signal that Islamabad was serious about fighting Islamic extremism and was expecting to be welcomed by Western leaders.

Waziristan, which runs along the Afghan border, was a possible hiding place for Osama bin Laden. It was also a place where, according to the British intelligence services, many plots against Western targets are hatched. Owais Ghani, governor of North West Frontier Province, the top civilian official responsible for the tribal area, did not mince his words: 'The military and law enforcement agencies have been ordered to carry out a full-fledged operation to eliminate these beasts and killers by using all resources'. He continued, stating that Baitullah Mehsud, leader of the Taliban in the region, 'is the root cause of all evils'. Ghani added, 'The move follows the Pakistan army's operation against a branch of Mehsud's Taliban network in the Swat Valley, which started in late April that year'.

Waziristan, however, is a much tougher nut to crack. The terrain, as we have seen, is difficult, and presents many problems to the Pakistan security forces launching an offensive. Pakistan is still struggling to cope with the displacement of about two million people from the Swat operation. Waziristan, in the northwest, could produce another half million refugees. Baitullah Mehsud's group claimed three major terrorist attacks: the bombing of a luxury hotel in Peshawar, a blast at a mosque in Nowshera in the North West, and the killing of an anti-Taliban cleric in the eastern city of Lahore. He is suspected of masterminding the assassination of Benazir Bhutto, the former prime minister, in 2007.

By the middle of October 2009 the ground offensive, long in the planning and long delayed, was under way - but the Taliban had expected the offensive and they struck back in the very heart of

Pakistan, in Lahore, Peshawar and Rawalpindi, partly to parade their strength, and partly to deflect attention from the government offensive. The attacks were audacious; the results greater than they dared have hoped.

Ever since July the Pakistan army had been preparing for an attack on Taliban power in Waziristan, held by Taliban, Uzbeks and Al Qaeda fighters. In the build-up to a ground offensive, enemy areas had been relentlessly shelled by artillery, with support from jet aircraft. Roads had been sealed off, partly to make it easier for troop movements, partly to prevent the escape of militants. Many civilians had been unable to leave the areas but that is one of the results of modern warfare that civilians become caught up in hostilities. War, as we have noted before, and as General William Tecumseh Sherman[40] originally said in 1880, is hell.

Then Mehsud's Taliban struck. Within hours of leaving their camps early on Saturday morning to fight what is being hailed as the decisive battle in the war against terror, 12 soldiers had been killed in the first ferocious gunfights. Pakistan's generals have called the offensive the 'mother of all battles' for the survival of a country under siege. There were reports of Taliban compounds coming under aerial bombardment from Pakistan gunships as troops moved out in three columns from Razmak to the north, Jandola to the east and Shakai in the west, and advanced on notorious Taliban target towns like Makeen and Ladha.

The significance of Pakistan's army having Makeen in its sights will

---

[40] General William Tecumseh Sherman (08 Feb 1820 – 14 Feb 1891) William Tecumseh Sherman was born to a prominent family in Lancaster, Ohio, on 8 February 1820, one of 11 children. His father, Charles Sherman, was a successful lawyer and Ohio Supreme Court justice and died when William was 9. In his memoirs, he wrote that his father gave him the name William Tecumseh because he admired the Shawnee chief. Educated at United States Military Academy, West Point. Early military career was a near disaster, having to be temporarily relieved of command. He returned at the Battle of Shiloh to victory and then gathered 100,000 troops destroying Atlanta and devastating Georgia in his March to the Sea. Often credited with the saying, "war is hell," he was a major architect of modern total war.

not have been lost on Pakistan's president, Asif Zardari. The late Taliban leader, Baitullah Mehsud, was in Makeen when he was allegedly recorded on a telephone intercept claiming responsibility for the assassination of Mr Zardari's wife, Benazir Bhutto, the former Pakistan prime minister. This remote and dusty town close to the Afghan border had expected as much. It was for many months the location chosen by the Americans for Predator drone attacks on Taliban commanders. It is in Makeen that there have been kidnappings of Pakistani troops, and fierce gun battles between security forces and militants. Thousands of residents had already fled the anticipated army assault, and those who remained were under military curfew. The long-awaited army ground offensive had started. Long delayed, as army generals agonised over how the country would cope with the militant backlash, which would inevitably follow. They had to weigh up the situation with great care. In fact, the backlash happened, as we have noted, even before the army assault.

The breakthrough came late on Friday night when, in a highly unusual move, the Chief of Army Staff at the time, General Ashfaq Kiyani, summoned all the main opposition party leaders to a meeting at the home of the Prime Minister, Yousuf Raza Gilani. Once assembled they were asked for united support for what would be one of the army's most controversial operations: the use of overwhelming force against their own people - many of them tribal militants who had once been trained and encouraged by some of the leaders and generals now moving against them. But after one of the bloodiest weeks in recent history, in which Taliban fighters had stormed the Army's Rawalpindi headquarters and more than 160 people were killed by suicide bombers and commando-style gunmen, the generals and the politicians had little choice.

It was the beginning of that same month, October 2009, when Sailab Mehsud, a local journalist covering Pakistan's dangerous tribal areas, received a call to meet the Taliban's new chief, Hakimullah Mehsud, at a secret location. (Hakimullah is a nom de guerre, but the Mehsud part is correct). He was immediately sure he was onto a scoop. Hakimullah was supposed to be dead.

According to Pakistani security forces, the militants' notorious 'boy general' (he was believed to be 28 years old or thereabouts) had been killed in a bitter succession battle with two rival Taliban commanders, Wali Ur Rahman and Qari Hussain. His 'death' had been a key factor in the army's preparations for a final assault. The Taliban had been wiped out in the Swat Valley, their South Waziristan leader, Baitullah Mehsud, had been killed in an American drone attack in August, and now they were in disarray. Would there ever be a better time to launch a massive offensive? But when the handful of journalists summoned by the Taliban awoke after an overnight stop deep in South Waziristan on 4 October, following an eleven hour mountain and forest drive, they were greeted by the smiling face of the 'dead' man, brandishing an AK-47 for the cameras and demonstrating with his laptop that he also has advanced computer skills. 'Tell the Pakistani government that I'm alive and determined to take severe revenge for Baitullah Mehsud's killing and the continued drone strikes', Hakimullah, told the reporters, urging them to record his message on film. 'Both America and Pakistan will have to face the consequences. We have respect for Al Qaeda and the jihadist organisations - we are with them'. He pledged to fulfil the mission of his predecessor to destroy the Pakistani state for its 'collaboration' with the West and drown the country in blood.

Within hours of this interview being broadcast on 5 October - Mehsud had insisted on a delay to give him time to disappear - the boy general delivered on his threat unleashing a wave of coordinated commando raids and suicide bombings which shattered any claims of Taliban disarray, and destroyed the notion that they would be easy prey in their South Waziristan stronghold.

The attacks began when a suicide bomber dressed as a paramilitary soldier tricked his way into a heavily guarded United Nations office in Islamabad and blew himself up killing five UN employees. On 9 October a car bomb ripped through a busy market place in Peshawar, the capital of the North West Frontier Province, killing 53 people.

The tipping point came in the third week of October 2009 the Pakistani Taliban and its extremist allies demonstrated the scale of their ambition. A team of 10 gunmen attacked the army's General Headquarters in Rawalpindi shooting their way through two gates to take 42 people hostage. In a 22-hour siege, which was fought out live on television, 14 soldiers and civilian employees were killed along with all but one of the terrorists. Such a brazen assault on the nerve centre of the country's military establishment heightened fears, not only in Pakistan but interested observers around the world, about the security of the country's nuclear weapons, if the army could be humiliated like this in its own headquarters.

This was not the end of the brazen assaults; it appeared Mehsud was just getting into his stride. Within days a child suicide bomber, no older than 13 years, targeted a military convoy moving through a bazaar in Shangla, close to the Swat Valley in the North West Frontier Province. The blast killed all six soldiers in an army vehicle and thirty-five shoppers on the street. Another myth was exploded - the notion that the Taliban had been totally defeated in Swat. Then came three simultaneous gun and explosives assaults in Pakistan's cultural and business capital Lahore, in the heart of Punjab. Commandos struck at two police training centres and the office of the Federal Investigation Agency, the national law enforcement body. The so-called 'swarm' attack was modelled on the 26 November attack in the previous year on Mumbai, and the death toll could have matched it had it not been for a fight-back from local security forces that limited the deaths to twenty-eight.

Meanwhile in Kohat, back in the North-West Frontier Province, another suicide bomber killed eleven on the same day when he rammed his car into a police station. Later that day a car exploded outside a housing complex for government employees in Peshawar killing a six-year-old boy and wounding nine others including women and children. On Friday the death toll climbed higher still when a car bomb exploded as it drove into the front of Peshawar's police intelligence headquarters. According to some unconfirmed reports one of the attackers was a woman who jumped from a motorbike, unbuttoned her coat, and detonated her suicide vest beside a neighbouring government housing complex and killing thirteen. Half the police station was completely destroyed by the blast and the other half engulfed in flames, while dazed police officers searched for their missing comrades in the rubble.

Ordinary Pakistanis have been left bewildered, unable still to believe that the danger comes from within their own country. 'Only

God knows where such people come from because I know that Muslims cannot kill other Muslims', said Mohammad Yousaf, a 55-year-old man who runs a tea shop near one of the police training schools in Lahore and spent several hours hiding inside his store as gunfire and explosions engulfed the area.

This latest Taliban onslaught, waged by leaders who were supposed to be dead, thoroughly shocked Pakistan. In fact, despite its omnipresent ISI (intelligence agency), and large standing army, it was the latter that appeared to be in the greatest disarray. Army headquarters had been left poorly guarded despite several Taliban attacks on military centres in the previous two years. The militants anticipated similar chaos when they decided to attack the same Lahore police training college they had laid siege to earlier in the year, and they were not disappointed.

The Army's top brass was reported to be furious, not only with the failings of their own people, but also with their political leaders. The country's interior minister at the time Mr Rehman Malik was virtually banned by generals from paying his respects to the dead at the army's GHQ. They blamed him for leaking their plans for the imminent South Waziristan offensive. Such leaks were of serious importance. They gave warning to Taliban fighters as well as Uzbek militants, Arabs and Mehsud tribesmen, who moved into neighbouring Orakzai in order to escape the military onslaught and thus live to fight another day. Not all fled, however; some stayed behind to put up a fight. An army convoy was bombed at Razmak, several soldiers were killed or wounded at Sarwakay and more were injured in a gun battle at Spinkay Raghzay - but the main battle was yet to be engaged.

For Pakistan's allies in the war on terror the army offensive may not materially assist their struggle against the Taliban across the border in Afghanistan. The army is targeting Taliban fighters from the Mehsud tribe, which have allied themselves with Al Qaeda in attacking Pakistan's military institutions. But the offensive is not expected to target the Haqqani network, a branch of the Taliban that has mounted some of the worst attacks on NATO forces in Afghanistan. Nor will it take on other pro-Afghan Taliban factions that support Mullah Omar's call for militants to focus their attacks on Western forces rather than the Pakistani military. Some observers blame Pakistan's ties with the United States; the jihadists now see no difference between the Americans and the Pakistan army. There are fears that the alliance with the United States will lead to the destruction of Pakistan as a state, little more than sixty years after its foundation at the partitioning of the sub-continent. To add substance to this claim is the knowledge that jihadists are not only in Waziristan, but are to be found in Punjab, Baluchistan, and in Sindh.

On how many fronts can the Pakistan army fight? Does it have the means to subdue its own Taliban rebels, to fight Afghan Taliban taking shelter in its country, and also keep control of Kashmir? When General Ashfaq Kayani called together members of the cabinet and leaders of opposition parties on 16 October 2009, he warned them to brace themselves for an unprecedented terrorist backlash. Without doubt, as the general made abundantly clear, Pakistan as a state is fighting for its very existence.

The taking of South Waziristan, which has not been achieved in days or even over many months, is important for several reasons. It is the main refuge for militants from Afghanistan. It also has numerous training camps for suicide bombers. Most importantly for Pakistan within this region, it is destabilizing Pakistan itself. Yet it is no easy decision for a general to issue orders for his soldiers to open fire on their own people.

Future policy for deciding a new government in Afghanistan needs to be purely on the lines of ratio of ethnicity, and Pashtuns are the major players. Even so, far more than the future government of Afghanistan, and far more than the outcome of the battle for South Waziristan is at stake. The stability and future of Pakistan and its place within the sub-continent are also of paramount importance. The fulcrum is Pakistan and Allied forces need to understand that they cannot afford another destabilized state in this region - particularly as Pakistan is a nuclear power and has a huge population. A destabilised Pakistan will certainly be more dangerous for the world. The Allied effort must take Pakistan into account, not merely as a client state, but as a full-time player in a sub-continental drama that is being played out in the cockpit of Asia.

Chapter 9

Proxy War

The conflicting interests of the regional powers led to another proxy war[41] in Afghanistan, with Pakistan, Saudi Arabia, and the United Arab Emirates supporting the Taliban, and Iran, Russia, and India supporting the Northern Alliance. As a result this war torn country is bleeding.

There is domination by Northern Alliance and Indian influence - after Masoud's assassination, Fahim being one of the vice presidents of Afghanistan, had become the main conduit for India's overt and covert assistance to the Northern Alliance in its struggle against the Taliban. Another of India's friends, in the interim administration, is Foreign Minister Abdullah Abdullah (present-day Prime Minister). India tried in vain, and even with help from the U.S., to bring Abdullah to power in the last presidential elections but somehow or another he was removed from the game. He is back again in power sharing formula as Prime Minister of the country, what does this mean? It is clear cut evidence that how much interest India and Iran are taking in controlling Afghanistan.

Regarding the Russo-Indo-Irani Nexus and the Great Game in Afghanistan - while the Taliban were in control of Afghanistan, India strove to form a common front with Iran, Russia, and the Central Asian Republics[42] against the religiously inspired 'terrorism' purportedly being propagated by Pakistan and the Taliban. This move, designed to reduce Pakistan's role in Central Asia, is the North-South Corridor Agreement, while connecting St Petersburg, via Tehran and Moscow.

Whilst defence and foreign affairs is in the firm grip of the

---

[41] proxy war - a war instigated by a major power that does not itself become involved.
[42] Central Asian Republics - the countries of Kazakhstan, Kyrgyzstan, Tajikistan, Turkmenistan, and Uzbekistan. Constituent republics of the former Union of Soviet Socialist Republics, they all achieved independence in late 1991.

Northern Alliance, Pakistan cannot possibly expect any diplomatic or material support from its western counterpart, in case war should break out with India. Indian consulates in the eastern cities of Afghanistan alongside Pakistan's western border are indeed posing a serious threat to the internal security of Pakistan in the form of propagating sectarianism (Shia-Sunni) and terrorism. Also, the fact that several members of the present Afghan government, including Hamid Karzai, have deep links with India in the shape of their education, (Karzai graduated from high school in Kabul in 1976 then travelled to India as an exchange student and attended Himachal Pradesh University), which means they will be moulded easily by India.

Another disquieting development for Pakistan is the nexus forged between India and Iran over Afghanistan. The two countries collaborated closely in propping up the Northern Alliance against Pakistan's interest.

There is a danger of prolonged insurgency and lawlessness in the FATA and Balochistan, Afghanistan geographical contiguous areas, which is making Pakistan destabilised.

The cost of the recent and comprehensive defeat in Afghanistan is yet to be calculated but, according to one assessment, the current war in Afghanistan is expected to inflict a direct cost on the Pakistan economy of more than US $10 billion.

In 2012, many top Afghan officials were assassinated mostly in night raids, including the mayor and police chief of Kandahar, and the brother of the U.S.-installed President Karzai.

To add to the toll of misery more than 3,000 U.S. and other NATO troops have been killed and more than 12,000 wounded so far, and many troops are suffering with catastrophic psychological trauma. An article in the Washington Post reported that U.S. military doctors now call double-leg amputations with accompanying genital injuries the 'signature wound' of the Afghanistan war.

In his article, dated 7 October 2011, entitled '10 Years, 10 Facts', and Mehdi Hasan reported, 'it is a time to reflect and deliberate. Here are ten important things about the conflict that are worth considering on this particular anniversary:

1. The British government has spent more than £18 billion on the

war in Afghanistan. Last year alone, the Treasury allocated £4 billion for the fight against the Taliban.

2. There have been 382 UK military fatalities[43] in Afghanistan since the start of operations in October 2001 – 35 of them this year. The UK military death toll in Afghanistan long ago exceeded the number of military casualties in the Falklands war (255) and the invasion of Iraq (179).

3. The average age of British casualties in Afghanistan is 22; 28 of those 382 dead soldiers were teenagers.

4. According to figures collated by the United Nations, the number of civilians killed in conflict in Afghanistan rose by 15 per cent in the first six months of this year to 1,462 non-combatants. Insurgents were held responsible for 80 per cent of the killings, with pro-government forces (including western forces) held responsible for 14 per cent of all civilian deaths.

5. The invasion of Afghanistan has not made the UK safer - the London bombings occurred four years after the commencement of military operations against the Taliban. On 7 July 2005, British troops were serving in Afghanistan when the four suicide bombers struck the capital's transport network. In fact, 7/7 bomber, Shehaz Tanweer, explicitly referred to British forces fighting in Afghanistan in his suicide video. As one of the UK's leading security experts, John Mackinlay of King's College, told me almost two years ago: 'Afghanistan is the recruiting sergeant for what is happening in the UK.

6. The U.S. and UK governments say we are fighting against al-Qaeda in Afghanistan – yet, as long ago as October 2009, Obama's (then) national security adviser, General James Jones, told CNN that 'the al-Qaida presence (in Afghanistan) is very diminished. The maximum estimate is less than 100 operating in the country. No bases. No ability to launch attacks on either us or our allies.'

---

[43] As at 30 April 2013- these figures rose according to the Ministry Of Defence (MOD) website Roll of Honour a total of 444 British forces personnel or MOD civilians have died while serving in Afghanistan since the start of operations in October 2001 and these figures have continued to rise.

7. The Taliban is a brutal, reactionary and despotic movement but it isn't a terrorist group, international or otherwise, and nor does it pose a direct or imminent threat to British national security. None of the 19 hijackers on 9/11 were Afghans or members of the Taliban. Of the dozen or so major terror plots that UK security agencies have successfully prevented since 11 September 2001, none have been linked to Afghanistan. Of the 100 or so Islamists imprisoned in Britain on terrorism offences, not a single one hails from Helmand.

8. Our chief ally in Afghanistan, Hamid Karzai, has been described by senior U.S. officials in internal diplomatic cables as "not an adequate strategic partner" who "continues to shun responsibility for any sovereign burden", is "paranoid, "weak", and has "an inability to grasp the most rudimentary principles of state-building". Peter Galbraith, who served as a UN envoy to Afghanistan until 2009, has since publicly questioned the "mental stability" of Karzai and even suggested that the Afghan president may be using drugs. In April 2010, Karzai threatened to quit politics and join the Taliban if the west put any further pressure on him to reform his government. I have referred to him elsewhere as Afghanistan's Ngo Dinh Diem.[44]

9. Britons oppose the war in Afghanistan by a 2-to-1 margin. The majority, 60 per cent, of the public opposes the war in Afghanistan, while only a minority, 31 per cent, supports it. It is the same across the pond: the overwhelming majority of Americans, 73 per cent, are in favor of withdrawing troops from Afghanistan.

10. For the past decade, western governments have repeatedly claimed that the war in Afghanistan was justified by the Taliban's refusal to hand over Osama bin Laden for trial. This is a lie. The *Daily Telegraph* reported on 4 October 2001, three days before the bombing began that a once secret plan to put Osama bin Laden on trial in Pakistan was blocked after President Musharraf said he could not guarantee his safety. Suggested by the Taliban's closest allies in Pakistan, it was a last-ditch attempt to satisfy Western demands for

---

[44] Ngo Dinh Diem - the pro-US president of South Vietnam, hailed by Lyndon Johnson as the "Churchill of Asia" but then executed by his own generals in 1963, with American approval, after his thuggish and corrupt behaviour exacerbated the Vietcong insurgency.

bin Laden's surrender while averting a war and ensuring the fanatical regime's survival. A high-level delegation led by Qazi Hussain Ahmad, head of Pakistan's most important Islamic party, the Jamaat-i-Islami, met Mullah Omar, the Taliban leader, in secret. Omar agreed that bin Laden should be taken to Pakistan, where he would be held under house arrest in Peshawar. The proposal, which had bin Laden's approval, was that within the framework of Islamic Sharia law evidence of his alleged involvement in the New York and Washington attacks would be placed before an international tribunal. The court would decide whether to try him on the spot or hand him over to America.

Ten long and bloody years later and bin Laden is now dead; Al Qaeda is scattered; Pakistan is on the verge of implosion; the U.S. government is in talks with the Taliban - and yet still we continue to send British troops to fight and die in the killing fields of Afghanistan. It is one of the great tragedies and scandals of our times.'

Chapter 10

So What Can The United States of America Do Now?

According to many sources America's debt has crossed more than 17 trillion dollars. At this crucial time period when health, education and other vital government programs are being slashed or eliminated altogether, thousands of Americans are jobless, people have become bankrupt, and the war in Afghanistan consumes millions of dollars per day. A report from a recent study by the prestigious Harvard University's Kennedy School of Government estimated that more than a decade-long American wars in Afghanistan and Iraq would end up costing as much as $6 trillion ($6,000,000,000,000) the equivalent of $75,000 for every American household The authors have also warned that the legacy of decisions taken during the Iraq and Afghanistan wars would dominate future federal budgets for decades to come. According to the Harvard University report, some 1.56 million U.S. troops - 56 per cent of all Afghanistan and Iraq veterans - were receiving medical treatment at Veterans Administration facilities and would be granted benefits for the rest of their lives. It further reveals, 'One out of every two veterans from Iraq and Afghanistan has already applied for permanent disability benefits. The official figure of 50,000 American troops wounded in action vastly underestimates the real human costs of the two U.S. wars. One-third of returning veterans are being diagnosed with mental health issues - suffering from anxiety, depression, and post-traumatic stress disorder (PTSD).' The report notes that in addition, over a quarter of a million troops have suffered traumatic brain injuries (TBI), which, in many cases, were combined with PTSD, posing greater problems in treatment and recovery. The same report has estimated, 'While the U.S. government has already spent $134 billion on medical care and disability benefits for Iraq and Afghanistan veterans, this figure will climb by an additional $836 billion over the coming decades.' It notes that the largest expenditures on health care for World War II veterans took place in the 1980s, roughly four decades after the war, and that spending on medical care and disability payments for Vietnam War veterans was still on the rise.

The only way to end the bloody and rising carnage in Afghanistan is to immediately withdraw all U.S. and NATO troops and aircraft. The timeline for U.S. withdrawal from Afghanistan was recently made quite clear - 10,000 troops out by the end of 2012 and 23,000 more out by the end of 2013. The remaining troops, if all goes according to plan, will be withdrawn before the end of 2014, with a possible residual assistance force of unspecified size thereafter.

That solves the military equation, but what about the political formula? How will Afghanistan itself be governed after the 2014 withdrawal? Will the country remain under its current administration/government? What role will the Taliban play? How will power be dispersed between Kabul and the provinces? How about the role of neighbouring Pakistan? What will be the role given to Pakistan? The most important question arises here is what can the United States do to answers these questions? Naturally all stakeholders desire a win-win situation here and want to safeguard their own interests as much as possible.

President Obama while making the withdrawal announcement was remarkably silent on all these important questions. It is clear as usual that the U.S. primary interest in Afghanistan is to defeat Al Qaeda; on talking about governance in Afghanistan the President said only that it would not be 'perfect'. That is not much guidance for diplomats and aid workers, who are looking ahead to set the course for the coalition partner's withdrawal, as well as the Afghans for the short time remaining before completion of the withdrawal process.

The governments in Europe and of other coalition partners want to see political reconciliation and smooth withdrawal; this has become popular opinion in the U.S. as well. The recently retired Defense Secretary Robert Gates (who would no longer be involved in the process) who suggested that by the end of year 2012 was a reasonable timeframe for negotiations with the Taliban to begin yielding results.

So now what can we hope for by way of a political settlement, and what are the options? President Obama, in one of his announcements on Afghanistan, reiterated his goals for reconciliation negotiations with the Taliban: they must break with Al Qaeda, leave violence, and must accept the Afghan constitution. The Taliban leadership, most importantly the Haqqani network and Mullah Omar's party, show no sign of feeling compelled to comply with these demands. A few days afterward and presumably in response to the speech, Taliban members attacked the Intercontinental Hotel in Kabul, targeting Afghan politicians gathered to discuss the impending turnover of security responsibility for Kabul and several provinces to the Afghan National Security Forces. It is clear that at least some of the Taliban will fight on for a long time, as insurgents in Iraq have done.

Some Taliban, however, may want a deal, and the German government has been hosting talks aimed at such a settlement. What might the Taliban hope to gain in return for meeting something like the President's deadlines? So far, the focus seems to have been on confidence-building measures like freeing prisoners and removing Taliban from terrorist lists. Washington does not like to discuss it, but an overall political settlement will only be possible if the Taliban get something more substantial in return. The options are few - a share of political power in Kabul, control over territory, economic benefits, and guarantees of U.S. withdrawal.

Sharing political power in Kabul is not an easy fix. The Taliban fought a ferocious civil war against the Northern Alliance and other politicians who today govern in Kabul, having thrown the Taliban out of Kabul with U.S. assistance in 2001. The Taliban would want to reintroduce their version of strict religious practices, a move many in Kabul would resist. The Northern Alliance, many women, secularists, and others would not want to see the Taliban back in power in Kabul. The former presidential candidate (present Prime Minister) Abdullah Abdullah and former intelligence chief Amrullah Saleh have become the leaders of this rejectionist front. It will not be enough for the U.S. to approve Taliban political involvement; these Afghan groups would also need to be included.

Another option would be sharing power at the provincial level, especially in the more Pashtun provinces of the south and east. Afghanistan has only rarely been effectively ruled from Kabul. The Taliban could dominate politics in Helmand, Kandahar, and other provinces along the border with Pakistan, thus allowing the group its long-desired role in government without handing over the whole of Afghanistan. This could lead to a virtual partition of the country with the Taliban-dominated provinces becoming a de facto part of Pakistan. Some might even say this is good. It would give Pakistan the strategic depth it seeks in Afghanistan, reducing its incentives to continue meddling and promoting militancy, and prevent New Delhi from exploiting its relationship with Kabul to the detriment of Islamabad, at least in the border provinces.

There are only three assets of real economic value in Afghanistan: control over drug production and trade, control over mineral resources, and control over border crossings and transport. The Taliban already exercise a good deal of control of all three in parts of the countryside where they are dominant. The U.S. is not likely to gain enough control over drugs to interest the Taliban. To effectively exploit mineral resources would require a national mining and export framework and guarantees to foreign investors that only the government in Kabul can provide. If Afghanistan is to prosper then border crossings and transport will also need to be mainly under national control.

Finally, the Taliban have sought the complete withdrawal of foreign forces from Afghanistan. This is a problem. President Karzai has made it clear that he would like one or more American bases to remain in Afghanistan after 2014, and talks have begun on a strategic framework that would enable American forces to stay, provided the Afghan government asks them to do so. Washington wants such bases so that it will have the capability to strike against Al Qaeda, either in Afghanistan or Pakistan. The Taliban must fear that the Americans will use any residual presence to strike at them as well as to bolster Karzai's government.

The bottom line is that the Taliban may well feel they can gain more by fighting on than by negotiating, but if they get serious about negotiations they will likely seek a share of power in the south and east, along with some representation in Kabul. Political power is likely to bring some economic benefits as well, in particular control over border crossings and transport. The Taliban would also continue to control at least some drug production and trade where they are politically dominant. This is an unattractive proposition, especially for Afghan women and the Northern Alliance. It would most likely resemble Hizbollah's role in Lebanon, which has been a source of regional instability in the Middle East for many years. Is there anything that can be done that would amount to more than putting lipstick on this pig? The answer is yes, but it requires the U.S. to worry about something it has studiously ignored for many years - the Durand line[45], which is the border between Afghanistan and Pakistan that Pakistan accepts but Afghanistan does not. It is hard to find any two countries without an agreed and demarcated border that live happily side by side. When the question was posed to a national security advisor in Kabul years ago, why Afghanistan had not recognized the Durand line, he responded, 'I wouldn't want to foreclose options for future generations'. Pakistan is a country that lives with what it considers an existential threat from India to the south and east. It surely does not need another threat, however remote, on its western border. Ethnic Pashtun irredentism (the Pashtuns live on both sides of the Durand line) greatly complicates Islamabad's challenges.

Afghan recognition of the Durand line as part of a broader deal with the Taliban would provide Pakistan with an important benefit, without depriving it of strategic depth inside Afghanistan. This would have to be done in a way that allows a good deal of freedom of movement across the border otherwise the Taliban and other locals, who have enjoyed relatively free movement for decades would object. But agreeing to and demarcating the Durand line would markedly improve relations between Kabul and Islamabad, enabling them to collaborate on what really counts for the U.S., ensuring that their border area does not become a haven for international terrorists.

---

[45] The Durand Line (Pashto: د ډیورنډ کرښه) refers to the 2,640 kilometers (1,640 mi) long porous border between Afghanistan and Pakistan. It was established after an 1893 agreement between Sir Mortimer Durand of British India and Afghan Amir Abdur Rahman Khan for fixing the limit of their respective spheres of influence as well as improving diplomatic relations and trade. It is named after Sir Mortimer Durand, K.C.I.E., a British diplomat and civil servant of colonial British India. The British considered Afghanistan an independent princely state at the time, although the British controlled its foreign affairs and diplomatic relations.□□□

President Hamid Karzai stated in the recent past that Afghanistan is ready right now to take all security responsibilities completely. Seemingly in response to this claim the West is systematically withdrawing its troops from Afghanistan. Of paramount importance is the need to accomplish the withdrawal in the most expeditious manner while still providing for the safety of the troops. But should the United States Government also withdraw its foreign aid? There is little Constitutional support for providing such aid other than an extremely strained interpretation of how it might impact the 'general Welfare of the United States' (Constitution of the United States Of America[46], under Article I, Section 8). If the U.S. is to respect the sovereignty of a foreign country then surely it cannot be selective in this regard. Of course this would not preclude private citizens from exercising their right to provide charitable contributions to other countries either directly or through the Non-Government Organization, but it reflects the fact that it is not the responsibility of, nor even the authority of the United States Government to use their own taxpayers' money to support the citizens of other sovereign nations.

Every country should have the right to evolve at its own pace rather than at the rate deemed appropriate by others, and moreover, based upon the interloper's own ideology. Some may see this as an uncaring approach but if the American people truly believe what their own Declaration of Independence[47] states, '...that all men are created equal, endowed by their Creator with certain unalienable Rights, that

---

[46] Constitution Of The United States of America - The fundamental law of the United States. It was framed by a convention of the representatives of the people, who met at Philadelphia, and finally adopted it on the 17th day of September 1787. It became the law of the land on the first Wednesday in March 1789.

[47] The Declaration of Independence is a statement adopted by the Continental Congress on July 4, 1776, which announced that the 13 American colonies, then at war with Great Britain, regarded themselves as independent states, and no longer a part of the British Empire. Instead they formed a union that would become a new nation - the United States of America.

among these are Life, Liberty and the pursuit of Happiness', then the U.S. must respect the Liberty (rights) of all citizens of other sovereign nations to pursue their own Happiness (welfare) in such a way as they choose to define it. In the case of Afghanistan, President Karzai's government must be given every opportunity to succeed or fail on its own merit.

According to T.J. O'Hara[48] who talks about the 'freedom process' in his article in *The Washington Times*, March 20, 2012 entitled Foreign policy: A rational approach for the U.S., 'This is not a xenophobic approach but rather a celebration of the richness of the world's diversity. There are 196 to 258 different countries in the world (depending on one's definition of the word "country"). Each one reflects its own unique culture, political structure and socio-economic system. We should have no expectation of imposing our will upon them. In turn, those who reject the United States' culture, political structure, and socio-economic system have a wide variety of other countries in which they can pursue 'Happiness' as they personally prefer to define it. Moreover, US Constitution does not provide direct guidance in the area of foreign policy. It wasn't until 1936 that the Supreme Court decided that the Federal Government had exclusive and plenary power over the execution of foreign affairs based upon the fact that the United States is a sovereign nation. Building upon that premise, I suggest extending the concept of sovereignty to every other nation as the foundation of our foreign policy. That decision alone will provide a consistency that is sorely lacking in a U.S. foreign policy that is all too often driven by Party politics.'

O'Hara affirms the need for the U.S. to develop a rational and stable foreign policy solution for Afghanistan moving forward, 'rather than one that fluctuates with any political opportunity that is presented', and accordingly to look beyond the foreign policy effect of applying the sovereign nations approach to Afghanistan, at the multi-faceted issues and make a non-partisan assessment of the opportunities - these issues would represent: resource policy,

---

[48] T.J. O'Hara - former independent candidate for the Office of President of the United States with a strong Constitutional background and extensive private sector experience as a chief executive and turnaround expert.

economic policy, education policy, defense policy, operations policy, medical policy - and to assess the impact.

Resource Policy impact - the withdrawal of U.S. troops from Afghanistan would have a direct influence on national energy and environmental issues. The Department of Defense (DoD) is the single largest consumer of fuel in the United States and in the world. A significant share of that consumption is attributable to troop logistics and the operation of vehicles and crafts in foreign lands. Withdrawing U.S. troops from Afghanistan would lead to a quantifiable reduction in the military's carbon footprint and contribute favorably to the environment, and would create a noticeable decrease in the DoD's demand and consumption of fuel. In turn this would trigger significant economic savings.

Economic Policy impact - withdrawing the troops from Afghanistan would have a significant positive economic impact on everyone in America. The operating cost of the wars in Iraq and Afghanistan rapidly approached trillion in recent years, and counting. While the U.S. has technically withdrawn from Iraq the country continues to incur costs in Iraq on a daily basis. As an ongoing theatre of war Afghanistan accounts for about $512 billion of this total and continues to drain capital from the American purse at a rate of around $300 million per day. While not all of that money could be recouped through the withdrawal of troops, those numbers do not reflect the related costs that are incurred in America, which are estimated to be at least on a par. So the potential savings to the taxpayer could indeed be considerable. If the U.S. Congress and incumbent administration acts responsibly then some of the money saved might be used to reduce debt, while the remainder could be deployed to build new, and/or expand existing military bases to welcome home and host returning troops. The latter utilization would create much needed construction jobs, and in turn lower unemployment costs, and thereby will stimulate much needed growth in the economy.

The recent rate of fuel consumption is roughly 10,000 barrels per day (3.64 million barrels per year). Any meaningful reduction of that amount would have a significant effect on supply-side economics, which has the potential to measurably impact by lowering fuel prices for American citizens. To provide some perspective for those who are unfamiliar with the logistical costs associated with maintaining a military presence overseas, Pentagon officials testified before the House Appropriations Defense Subcommittee that in 2009 a gallon of fuel cost the DoD about $400 by the time it was delivered to the remote locations of U.S. troops in Afghanistan.

Education Policy and probable impact - the withdrawal of U.S. troops from Afghanistan would also have a potential supply-side impact on the American education system. Many of the returning troops are likely to return to school and an increase in the student population would help Spread University and trade school operating costs across a wider base. It would also increase the use of infrastructure in a way that would accelerate the payback period and increase the long-term return on investment for the institutions.

Defense Policy and probable impact - withdrawing the troops from Afghanistan would obviously reduce the operating expenses of the DoD. While some troops will leave the military, but those who remain in uniform need to be based somewhere and need to maintain a state of readiness for redeployment. The U.S. would have the opportunity to redeploy them along North America's northern and southern borders and to maintain their state of readiness by patrolling those same borders. This would not only accomplish the DoD's military imperative, it would help address the long-standing problems associated with eliminating or dramatically reducing the threats of terrorist infiltration, drug trafficking and illegal immigration. The border redeployment might also require new bases to be built and/or existing bases to be expanded and any related construction activity would create job growth, lower unemployment costs and stimulate economic expansion.

Operations Policy and probable impact - the withdrawal of troops from Afghanistan and redeploying them along U.S. borders would offer certain opportunities to improve the operating efficiency and cost effectiveness of Federal Government. After 9/11 the Bush Administration created new layers of agencies (Transport Security Agency, Department of Homeland Security, etc.,) to improve communications with respect to domestic threats. All this achieved throughout the intervening decade was the creation within these bureaucratic agencies of tens of thousands of new jobs, promulgating tens of thousands of pages of new regulations, costing tens of billions of dollars in implementation, and culminating in a relatively modest impact the security of the nation. They were however effective in creating more jurisdictional issues between agencies such as who was responsible for what (i.e., the DoJ's[49], the FBI's[50], the ATF's[51], the DEA's[52], the TSA's[53], the DHS's[54], the INS's[55], the FEMA's[56], etc.?). Meanwhile drug trafficking has expanded to a multi-billion dollar industry with money flowing out of the U.S. to Mexico and the border remains porous for almost anyone wanting to enter the country illegally from that country. If returning troops were positioned along the borders America would surely have the most efficient and effective defense team using the most sophisticated surveillance capabilities at its disposal, the jurisdictional issues would no longer get in the way of creating a secure border, and the numbers of agencies could be consolidated, and border-related intelligence

---

[49] Department of Justice - the United States federal department responsible for enforcing federal laws (including the enforcement of all civil rights legislation).

[50] Federal Bureau of Investigation - an agency of the Justice Department responsible for investigating violations of Federal laws.

[51] (Federal Bureau of) Alcohol, Tobacco and Firearms (abbreviation ATF) - the law enforcement and tax collection agency of the Treasury Department that enforces federal laws concerning alcohol and tobacco products and firearms and explosives and arson.

[52] Drug Enforcement Administration - federal agency responsible for enforcing laws and regulations governing narcotics and controlled substances; goal is to immobilize drug trafficking organizations.

[53] Transport Security Agency - an agency established in 2001 to safeguard United States transportation systems and insure safe air travel.

[54] Department of Homeland Security - the federal department that administers all matters relating to homeland security.

[55] Immigration and Naturalization Service - an agency in the Department of Justice that enforces laws and regulations for the admission of all foreign-born nationals to the United States.

[56] Federal Emergency Management Agency - an independent agency of the United States government that provides a single point of accountability for all federal emergency preparedness and mitigation and response activities.

gathering and enforcement centralized within the DoD. Looking at it this way the increased safety of American citizens as well as the potential economic savings is almost beyond comprehension, and the economic savings can be magnified by the societal gains associated with controlling U.S. borders. Consider the subsequent reduction in law enforcement, judicial and prison costs, the impact on the nation's health, education and welfare systems, the effect on the nation's job market, and so on. If the enormous waste is not enough to astound you, then perhaps consider the cost to the taxpayer associated with the DoJ's prosecution of States that are trying to supplement the Federal Government's failed enforcement, not to mention the waste of money at the State-level associated with drafting and defending any associated legislation and providing for auxiliary law enforcement. The cost of maintaining the United States military in a state of readiness would be one fixed cost.

Medical Policy and probable impact - there are appreciable and favorable medical consequences of withdrawing troops from Afghanistan. The U.S. has lost around 1,900 U.S. troops in Afghanistan; 16,000 more have been wounded and it is difficult to assess how many more have returned home suffering from post-traumatic stress disorder (PTSD), and this number is likely to be high since more returning veterans commit suicide each year than are killed in combat. There has been vast improvements in prosthetics devices and therapy to the degree that more of the injured are able to return to productive lives than in the past; but this should not detract from the reality that far too many young people are suffering life changing consequences as a direct result of the U.S.'s continued presence in Afghanistan. Consider the cost associated with ongoing care, and the cost associated with ancillary medical conditions that might arise in the future. Most importantly, consider the cost to the individuals themselves and to their families and friends.

There is an increasingly prevalent public sentiment that Afghanistan is becoming another Vietnam for the U.S. The puppet President, Hamid Karzai won election second time (albeit with charges of vote rigging), but he does not enjoy much popular support. Many call him rather derogatorily the 'Mayor of Kabul' as his governance is limited to the capital city. Instead warlords rule the roost in Afghanistan and a recent UN report suggests that drug dealers have been transformed into professional drug cartels. Both the Taliban together with rogue elements in the Afghan government support drug dealers because they are a major source of income. The Taliban, who are ethnic Pashtuns, are also successful in fueling sentiments of anti-Americanism by exploiting the poor performance of Karzai's government. Over fifty per cent of Afghanistan's population is Pashtun yet these people hardly enjoy a major political representation; though Karzai is an ethnic Pashtun the remainder of the Afghan government is Tajiks and Uzbeks (part of the Northern Alliance) who represent barely 25-30 per cent of the Afghan people.

As I have stated already the U.S. initially depended on the support of the Northern Alliance in invading Afghanistan. They treated Pashtuns as traitors and terrorists and launched massive operations against them. Although these military offensives were aimed against the Taliban, the Pashtun population got the distinct impression of mass genocide. Pakistani intelligence agencies, which some believe were covertly supporting the Taliban, encouraged such emotions, while playing host to hundreds of Taliban and Al Qaeda operatives. The Pakistani military establishment has been accused of deceiving the U.S. by giving the impression that they are front-line allies against the war on terror. Indeed, the Bush administration prodded Pakistan for its apparent double standards but failed to extract any positive commitment; Pakistanis did launch some operations to root out Taliban but failed to capture the top leadership - there are reports of tip-offs by some rogue elements in the Pakistani military. The Taliban 'guests' apparently started biting back at their hosts by launching a massive campaign of Islamic militancy in the North Western Province of Pakistan; they effectively control more than one-third of that province which the Pakistani military has failed to constrain.

Pakistani support for the Taliban along with some strategic mistakes of the Bush administration has now resulted in the biggest quagmire since the Vietnam War. Cheney-inspired Afghan policy relied on the support of the Northern Alliance and a suppression of Pashtun elements; a policy that already showed signs of failure in 2005 when the American troops launched a massive offensive against the Taliban. They failed to engage the Pashtuns in the Afghan political process and this estrangement helped the Taliban win sympathy among the majority of the population.

Nearly six months into the surge in Afghanistan and six months prior to the White House review of the Afghan war strategy, it was clear the U.S. mission in Afghanistan was not only failing but could even be beyond repair. The surge's goal was intended to blunt the Taliban's advance within the year and force it to negotiate from a position of weakness. But, rather than being weakened, once again the Taliban appears to be on ascent and will most likely continue to rise in popularity, according to a recent U.S. Defense Department assessment which indicates that most of Afghanistan's key 121 districts are neutral or sympathetic toward the Taliban, or even staunchly support it. Meanwhile, the Taliban has stymied efforts to establish the Afghan government's writ in the restive south, the Taliban heartland and the centre of gravity of this war. I think US has forgotten that Taliban which belongs to Pashtun tribe have been traditional rulers in Afghanistan and makes more than half of Afghan population. Practically without bringing them into loop of power peace is just a dream.

The Obama administration adopted a new and different Afghan policy that would address the Taliban issue through another surge in American troops, up to 21,000 in total. The policy came under fire even before its implementation; the biggest objection came with the report submitted by General Stanley McChrystal, the top U.S commander in Afghanistan at that time, which stated that any additional troops were not needed; instead, recruitment and training of Afghan forces would be enough to tackle the Taliban. The Obama administration also needs to get tough with the Indians, as Indian intelligence agencies are still supporting the factions operating against Taliban. They are getting huge economic assistance from India. An economically weak Pakistani establishment needs to stop its covert support for the Taliban and its obsession with India, it can only happen when India stop interfering in internal affairs of Afghanistan. If both of these countries stop their so-called national interest strategies, there is a possibility that the situation in Afghanistan may improve. Afghanistan is at the moment battleground for neighbours who are pursuing their interests. The only thing required here is a strong political will and President Obama has no lack of that.

The only solution to the Afghanistan problem is a mass diplomatic engagement with the Taliban leadership, excluding their very top leaders. If they were offered plenty of money and increased participation in Afghan politics then second and third-tier Taliban leaders might well be wooed, and, if their support can be won, they might also assist in capturing the top Al Qaeda leadership. Only a political solution can bring about lasting peace to Afghanistan and expeditiously remove the U.S. from this sordid conflict. Given Washington's bleak military predicament, sooner rather than later they must begin to offer precedence to a political reconciliation process with the senior Taliban leadership.

The recent U.S. concession to a plan for accepting division of political power in Afghanistan by the country's presidential candidates, Dr Abdullah Abdullah and his rival, Dr Ashraf Ghani Ahmadzai, following the controversial presidential polls in the country, has revived hopes about possible reduction in tensions and disputes. In his first public speech addressed to his supporters, Abdullah described the power sharing formula as the best option under the current sensitive conditions for his country and noted that it also conformed to the country's constitution as well as the good and expediency of Afghanistan and its people.

Truthfully, the election deadlock, which continued for a period of six months, offered limited options as to the way out of the crisis, which if rejected, the country's election turmoil would have simply worsened. Out of all options available to the two sides the following three were taken more seriously:
1. The establishment of a parallel government by Abdullah in case he failed to achieve an agreement with his rival.
2. The continuation of Hamid Karzai's government and arranging a re-election.
3. That of reconciliation.

Reconciliation was the only option recognised to be the best. It also gained domestic, regional and international support in the last steps of the dispute and through mediation of the United States'

Secretary of State John Kerry. The other two options could have led Afghanistan into domestic war and possible disintegration along ethnic and regional lines. We have to wait and see what will be the outcome of this, which will be quite clear in the near future.

This power structure and the federal system of government in Afghanistan will regard ethnic lines. It is also compatible with a plan previously proposed by the former head of foreign troops in Afghanistan General David Patraeus. According to Petraeus's plan the Pashtun ethnic group would be allowed to establish its own Islamic system of power in the eastern and western parts of the country where it commands a majority and would have a share of the central power in Kabul as well, provided that its people lay down their arms. The same formula would be extended to the other three major ethnic groups, which include Tajiks, Uzbeks, and Hazara people and as a result Afghanistan would turn into a federal country where the distribution of power would be more balanced.

A very important aspect within the power-sharing formula is a Loya Jirga to meet within the next two years to amend the country's constitution in such a way that it would meet the two main demands put forth by Abdullah Abdullah. Possible amendments in the Constitution of Afghanistan will take place along these two major lines. They will either turn the country's political system from a centralised presidential system into a non-centralised parliamentary system while the chief executive will be promoted to Prime Minister; or, the country's administrative system will be a federal one in which every ethnic group will have its own ethnic parliament and local government within its geographical boundaries and will also be given a fair share of power in Kabul.

Chapter 11

New Equations in Afghan Stability

After the U.S./NATO withdrawal Afghanistan's neighbours will have a major growing role to play in the country's stability. With Afghanistan's recent presidential election in turmoil or even power sharing formula is being implemented and on the table. The main issue the new president/prime minister will need to address, though, is the Bilateral Security Agreement (BSA) with the U.S., which the incumbent Hamid Karzai has determinedly refused to sign, despite extensive pressure from the U.S. and the looming pull-out of the International Security Assistance Force (ISAF). Karzai's stance may seem mysterious, especially since the BSA was endorsed by a Loya Jirga in November 2013. But he may be making a pragmatic judgment as to Washington's long-term ability to keep the peace in Afghanistan. The "Zero Option" (withdrawal of all troops by end 2014) that Washington has articulated, if implemented, will create a power vacuum in Afghanistan. Even if that option were avoided and a limited American force of approximately 5000 to 10,000 were maintained, there would still be a steep drop in area dominance capabilities, with Afghan National Security Forces left almost entirely in charge. The unhappy Taliban would undoubtedly attempt to fill the vacuum. Equally certain, Afghanistan's neighbours would not be comfortable with a radical Taliban exporting terror to their countries across porous borders. Even those that do not share borders with Afghanistan would be concerned. What role might these countries play in the wake of the NATO drawdown?

Iran

Among Afghanistan's more powerful neighbours is Iran. A Shia-majority nation, it feels a sense of responsibility for the considerable Shia population in Afghanistan. The two countries also share ethnic and linguistic overlaps. Iran's concern for the Shia of Afghanistan is evidenced in its past responses. Following the 1979 Russian takeover and Afghan resistance, Iran provided support for the Persian-speaking Shia groups. When the Taliban came to power, Iranians supported the Northern Alliance partners. In 1998, when the Taliban overran Majar-e-Sharif and massacred thousands of Hazaras and ten Iranians with diplomatic papers, Iran deployed its Army along its borders with Afghanistan.

Iran also faces a serious drug problem, with Afghan opium smuggled across its borders. Moreover, it hosts more than two million Afghan refugees.

In the recent past Iran has sought to increase influence primarily through economic avenues. It has built new roads, improved infrastructure, and provided concessions enabling Afghans access to Chabahar Port, allowing Kabul to avoid relying solely on Karachi. A railway link connecting Afghanistan with Iran and Tajikistan is under construction. Afghanistan has agreed to a friendship and cooperation pact with Iran.

Iran's deepening involvement in Afghanistan will undoubtedly not be welcome in all sections of Afghan society as well as internationally, significant conflict can be anticipated. However, progress with the interim agreement on Iran's nuclear program has improved its image in the U.S. and NATO countries, which may be more willing to accept a greater Iranian role in Afghanistan.

Central Asian Republics

The Central Asian Republics (CARs) have deep interests and substantial stakes in Afghan stability. For those that share borders with Afghanistan the most important issue is radical outfits potentially exporting terror and fundamentalism to their countries? There are also sizeable ethnic minority groups in Afghanistan with strong ties to the CAR. An Afghan government collapse would likely prompt an exodus of refugees to the CAR, creating economic, security and political problems. In the 1990s, the CAR attracted relatively few refugees; today, their better economic conditions make them attractive options for those wishing to flee a violent and unstable Afghanistan. Before the Taliban came to power in Kabul, the CAR extended economic aid to Kabul in a bid to provide stability. Today, while individually these countries may not be able to influence issues in Afghanistan decisively, they could contribute to a force under a UN flag, if such a force were deployed in Afghanistan.

China

China has up till now displayed only an economic interest in Afghanistan. Beijing is aware of the threat of an unstable Afghanistan and the possible destabilizing influence it could have in China's west. Its huge economy would be well served by the vast mineral deposits of Afghanistan, and China is presently pursuing infrastructure links through the neighbouring CAR countries, with rail and road projects already underway.

China always wanted to maintain a lower profile in Afghanistan, as ethnic differences and a lack of strong historical links may alienate the local populace. Chinese-funded projects in Myanmar employing large Chinese workforces have already faced similar situations. Beijing will also be quite happy with the U.S. footing the bill for Afghan stability, with or without the requisite boots on ground, while China draws on Afghan natural resources to fuel its growth.

According to David Sedney, a former U.S. diplomat in Beijing and Kabul and deputy assistant secretary of defence for Afghanistan, Pakistan and Central Asia from 2009 to 2013. "In a certain sense, they're competing with the U.S. for success in Afghanistan. They want to prove they can do it better,"

China has already taken the unusual step of a hosting a delegation of Afghan Taliban officials, creating a potential new avenue for peace negotiations between the insurgents and the government in Kabul. The December 2014 trip to Beijing by the Afghan Taliban delegation was the second in recent months, Afghan and foreign officials have already confirmed this - the visit came weeks after Afghan President Ashraf Ghani's visit to Beijing, his first official trip abroad.

The Taliban issued its first statement in January 2015 acknowledging contacts with China, but denied that Beijing was involved in peace talks. It said the recent Taliban delegation's visit to China was intended to build neighbourly relations. When it comes to political influence, China can deploy a swing of economic incentives while also leveraging what influence Pakistan has to achieve its objectives. However, China's position on Afghanistan has always mirrored Pakistan's, advocating a political role for the Taliban and a swift exit by U.S. troops.

The Chinese are likely to reap maximum benefits by concentrating in the economic investment sector. China is fast seizing a substantial share of Afghanistan's natural resources with the China Metallurgical Group Corp., Jiangxi Copper Corporation, and Zijin Mining Group Company winning a joint bid worth $3.5 billion meant to develop what's hyped to be the largest undeveloped copper field in the world. The Aynak copper field situated in the Logar province in central-east Afghanistan became the largest foreign direct investment in the history of Afghanistan, although tarnished by reports of corruption and bribery. According to estimates, the 28-square-kilometre Aynak copper field could contain up to $88 billion worth of ore in addition to other vital copper fields situated in Jawkhar and Darband in the relatively stable northern and north-western regions. Moreover, Afghanistan is home to large iron ore deposits stretching across Herat and the Panjsher Valley, and gold reserves in the northern provinces of Badakshan, Takhar and Ghazni. Employment opportunities for the Afghans has received a boost with the Chinese investment projects by virtue of electricity-generation projects for mining and extractions and a freight railroad passing from western China through Tajikistan and Afghanistan to Pakistan.

Pakistan

As far as Pakistan is concerned without any doubt they are the key players in whole issue and nobody should even think solving this issue without involving Pakistan. Whatever is the outcome of Afghan Presidential elections fraud Pakistan will remain deeply involved in Afghanistan. Its traditional philosophy of Afghanistan providing it strategic depth in a confrontation with India makes it imperative that any regime in Kabul be subservient to Islamabad. A stable Afghanistan with Kabul under its influence is central to Pakistan's Afghan strategy. If violence erupts on a large scale in Afghanistan, Tehrik-i-Taliban Pakistan, which has bases in Afghanistan, will need to relocate to the Northwest Frontier and Federally Administered Tribal Areas, exacerbating the problems Pakistan already faces.

Islamabad is reported to have advised the Karzai government to form stronger bonds with China. A China-Pakistan dominance with China pouring in the funds and Pakistan acting as the mentor for Kabul would suit Pakistani interests nicely.

Various types of propaganda is on the increase against Pakistan especially its intelligence agency ISI. Let me remind that it is the same agency through which United States fought proxy War with Russians and resultantly Russia collapsed. Operation Cyclone was the code name for the CIA's program to arm and finance the Afghan mujahedeen prior to and during the Soviet war in Afghanistan from 1979 to 1989. The program leaned heavily towards supporting militant Islamic groups that were favoured by neighbouring Pakistan because it was need for USA at the time. Operation Cyclone was one of the longest and most expensive covert CIA operations ever undertaken; funding began with $20–$30 million per year in 1980 and rose to $630 million per year in 1987. Funding continued after 1989 as the Mujahedeen battled the forces of Najibulla's People Democratic Party of Afghanistan (PDPA) during the Civil war in Afghanistan (1989-92). USA left Afghanistan after the downfall of Soviet Union leaving Pakistan and its Intelligence to deal with the aftermath of a long war. Pakistan accommodated Afghan refugees in millions and Kalashnikov culture prevailed all over Pakistan.

The ISI has been heavily involved in covertly running the military intelligence programs in Afghanistan since before the Soviet Invasion of Afghanistan in 1979. The 1980s saw systematically coordinated distribution of arms by the ISI and financial means provided by the CIA to some factions of the Afghan Mujahedeen. I strongly refute such types of propaganda against Pakistan but I would like to quote extracts from an article entitled "The ISI's Great Game in Afghanistan"[57] by Omar Aziz. "A widely held view in Pakistan's elite circles is that the U.S. will soon withdraw and leave the Afghan problem at Pakistan's doorstep. I have been hearing a variant of this view for five years now. With U.S. President Barack Obama's

---

[57] The ISI's Great Game in Afghanistan by Omar Aziz published 08 June 2014 available online at http://thediplomat.com/2014/06/the-isis-great-game-in-afghanistan

decision to leave 9,800 troops in Afghanistan through the end of 2014 and potentially leave zero troops after two years, it is apparent now that this view has not been unfounded. But Pakistan has wanted a vacuum in Afghanistan all along. A despoiled, anarchic vestige of a state to its east means that Pakistan can virtually control the territory, as it did through its various puppets throughout the 1980s and 1990s.

During the Soviet-Afghan War, American arms were shipped into Afghanistan through the ISI – Pakistani spymasters channelled funds and arms into the hands of their favourite militant groups, often the most retrogressive and extremist of the Mujahedeen. Leaders of some of these groups studied in Pakistani madrassas, a wellspring of indoctrination and militant thinking. By one estimate, the number of madrassas in Pakistan feeding the jihadists surged from 900 in 1971 to 32,000 in 1988. The ISI's strategy at the time – and which remains its strategy today – can be summed up by what Pakistani dictator Zia ul-Haq told his generals "Afghanistan must be made to boil at the right temperature."

Pakistan for its survival will have to contest any move by India to establish strong political and military influence in Afghanistan. The fear of being hemmed in by Indians to the East and an Afghan regime with Indian leanings to the West preoccupies the Pakistani establishment. Remember India is trying to settle its score with Pakistan and USA/NATO is providing that opportunity to Indians.

Russia

Russia will of course wish to avoid a rerun of its bitter experience in the 1980s. The fact that it no longer shares borders with Afghanistan dilutes its concern. Moscow will naturally be sensitive to insurgent groups based in Afghanistan developing adequate reach to find footholds in CAR countries that remain in Russia's orbit. Moscow is also on record as having stated its readiness to maintain Afghan military equipment.

India lacks the capability to field a large force in Afghanistan for any protracted period. Moreover, Pakistani opposition and the fact that India and Afghanistan do not share land borders rules out that option but instead heavy presence of RAW network within Afghanistan clearly shows Indian ambitions. India is trying to maintain a good image among Afghan citizens. If Iran plays or gets a major role in Afghanistan, India will have an opening to step up its role further. Indians and Chinese could also work together but that will not favour USA: Both countries want a piece of pie in Afghanistan - they have invested substantial capital in the country, and anticipate business opportunities with huge returns. New Delhi will for instance try helping to train Afghan forces.

The sudden deterioration of the situation in Ukraine raises issues of import for Afghanistan's future. The U.S. rebalancing to Asia, its deteriorating relationship with Russia, and the ongoing global war on terror barely permit it the resources to police Afghanistan as well. Western priorities are shifting, and the focus on Afghanistan is fading perceptibly. Combined with greater acceptance of Iran by Western powers and the steady rise of China, new equations in Afghanistan are all the more probable.

Afghanistan will in all likelihood require the deployment of outside forces to maintain stability after the ISAF withdrawal. Even if the zero option is not executed, and a force of approximately 3,000 or even 15,000 remains, the Taliban is likely to gradually expand the areas under its control. Neither the U.S. nor EU countries will have the appetite for another redeployment at that stage. The Russians will not want to get involved. With Indians out of contention and the Chinese unlikely to pursue anything beyond business interests, a multi-national force drawn primarily from regional countries may be the most viable option.

The dynamics of such a force would likely be stormy. Pakistan will want to dominate as there is no other option especially when India is trying to seize the country so that can be used against Pakistan. Due to various activities of RAW (Indian Intelligence) Pakistan's relations with Afghanistan are already full of tensions. Afghans blame Pakistan for many of the issues that trouble their nation. There are clear evidences, which shows active involvement of RAW against anti state activities within Pakistan via Afghanistan. Without a major role, Pakistan would have to play some sort of tactics; perhaps with more Indian contingent also taking the role. Consequently, if any multinational force operating in Afghanistan following the departure of the ISAF would perforce be mostly from the CAR, with possible contributions from Iran and definitely from India. In nutshell country will remain destabilize and nobody will be in a win win situation. USA and NATO has to understand and also has to take into account various concerns of neighbours especially Pakistan which has a border of more than 2000 km with Afghanistan.

India

Every country in the world pursues her national interests; some even at the cost of regional stability and peace. As the 2014 US withdrawal from Afghanistan is upcoming fast, every country in the region, i.e., Pakistan, India, Iran and China, is looking to secure their short and long term gains/interests in Afghanistan. At the moment, every regional country is devising a policy regarding how to move after the allied forces leave and the combat mission ends in Afghanistan. In this changing and emerging scenario, India is also looking for her interests in the region, particularly in Afghanistan. Besides huge Indian investment, reconstruction work, defence and security ties and training of Afghan National Security Forces, there is, somehow, an inevitable Indian presence in Afghanistan that is posing some serious questions and threats for regional peace and stability.

India's approach toward Afghanistan has largely been a function of the desire to prevent Pakistan from dominating that country, something Islamabad views as a vital counterweight to India's preponderance in South Asia. The two countries have been stuck in a classic security dilemma in so far as their Afghan policies are concerned, in that any measure by either side to increase its security is liable to trigger a reaction thus causing deterioration in the overall regional balance. Most important thing is that India has no direct borders with Afghanistan and making investments in billions of dollars is just to dominate any government operating in the country.

Afghanistan had expressed an urgent need for military hardware, particularly after a few skirmishes along its border with Pakistan. President Hamid Karzai, on his visits to India has presented a wish list consisting of T-72 battle tanks, 105 mm howitzers, An-32 transport aircraft, and Mi-17 helicopters along with bridge-laying equipment and trucks. Afghanistan has long expected assistance from India, making the case for mutual cooperation in the face of security threats from Pakistan.

India has placed a big arms order with Russia for Afghanistan, from Afghanistan's point of view, India's deal with Russia is a welcome move. The ISAF drawdown has left below 51,000 ISAF troops in the country, down from 140,000 in 2011. Both France and Canada ended their combat missions early and the UK has withdrawn from all but one Forward Operating Base in Helmand. Around 335 military bases across the country have been handed over to Afghan troops, according to a statement by the Military Bases Transition Commission. U.S. officials have recently resumed discussion on how many troops should remain in Afghanistan after this year. This number might drop below 10,000, the minimum demanded by the U.S. military to train Afghan troops.

To be very frank Afghanistan is going out of fashion among governments in the West, as attention shifts to a disintegrating Middle East and a new battlefront in Eastern Europe. But something may be moving in to fill the void. China and India held their first bilateral talks on Afghanistan in April 2013, and discussed the issue most recently during Xi Jinping's visit to New Delhi in September 2014. Both sides agreed to "strengthen strategic dialogue" on building "peace, stability and prosperity in Afghanistan," which was identified as a "shared interest."

China and India may not see eye to eye on many issues, but there is a growing convergence of interests in Afghanistan and the region. That both sides are willing to engage despite their tensions is commendable, and should be supported. As Western forces draw down in Afghanistan, a new China-India led regional multilateralism may be important in reenergizing the region and providing the opportunities for the prosperity and security that will underpin Afghanistan's future. Yet given that neither country is interested in security provision, these efforts are unlikely to be decisive – at least in the short-term. A solution to Afghanistan's problems must begin within the country, and a strong Western security commitment post-2014 will be just as important.

The Bottom Line

I would like to share an article entitled 'Afghanistan And The

Bottom Line' written by Jamie Tarabay 02 April 2014.

'In northern Afghanistan, a prison in Baghlan province built to house nearly 500 inmates is already falling apart - before it has even opened. Costing more than $11 million in American taxpayer money, it was built on a seismic fault line, without any safeguards. The construction, warns an independent government watchdog, is so bad at least one building has already been demolished. In a letter Wednesday to the State Department, John F. Sopko, the special inspector general for Afghanistan reconstruction, warned that, "any further construction using unsteady materials could threaten employee and prisoner safety and the security of the facility".

The alert from the office of the Special Inspector General of Afghanistan Reconstruction (SIGAR) is only the latest warning about questionable reconstruction spending in that country. Earlier this year, the agency issued a quarterly report detailing special projects funded by the State Department, the Defense Department and the U.S. Agency for International Development that it investigated and found to be incomplete, badly constructed or, in one case, not even wanted by the U.S. military.

As the United States begins to wind down its 13-year occupation of Afghanistan, an accounting of where the money has gone and whether it has been spent in a meaningful and substantive way is in full swing. The U.S. government has spent more than $80 billion on Afghanistan's reconstruction since it invaded the country in 2001. Half of that has gone to setting up and maintaining the country's police and military. Another $20 billion remains in the coffers amid concerns from both SIGAR and observers in Congress over how the money will be spent, whether the projects can be verified and even whether they can be sustained in a degenerating security environment with fewer U.S. troops on the ground expected by the end of the year.

"If anything, I tell people reconstruction becomes more important from a policy point of view," said Sopko. "Our stated policy for being there is to make certain Afghanistan never becomes a place where it can be a base for terrorist attacks against the United States and its allies." The U.S. military will largely be gone by 2015, he said, "so we've got to get Afghanistan reconstruction right if we really want to make a difference in the future".'

The U.S. has now spent more on the reconstruction of Afghanistan than it spent on the Marshall Plan, which resuscitated Europe after World War II, according to a special inspector general. The Marshall Plan delivered $103 billion in today's dollars to 16 European countries between 1948 and 1952. That has now been topped by congressional appropriations for reconstruction in Afghanistan, which so far have come to $109 billion in today's dollars. The difference being, The Marshall Plan helped Europe get back on its feet, while Afghanistan is a chaotic mess.

In a nutshell I think the U.S. must admit its mistakes and the only way to reconcile is to bring the Pashtuns into the mainstream politics of Afghanistan, and transfer of power according to ethnic group numbers.

Chapter 12

Way Forward: Suggestions and Recommendations

'Envisioning 2030: US Strategy for a Post-Western World' is a report of the Strategic Foresight Initiative at the Brent Scowcroft Centre on International Security. The Strategic Foresight Initiative is a practice area within the Atlantic Council's Brent Scowcroft Center on International Security that seeks to enhance understanding of the potential impact and the policy implications of long-term global trends, disruptive change, and strategic shocks.

Since its inception, the Atlantic Council has administered programs to examine political and economic as well as security issues, and to cover Asia, the Americas and other regions in addition to Europe. All its programs are, however, based on the conviction that a healthy transatlantic relationship is fundamental to progress in organizing a strong international system. The Atlantic Council Leadership Chairman from 2009-2013 was Senator Chuck Hagel who was, until recently, the Defense Secretary appointed by President Obama. As per this deliberate report United States think tanks have clearly defined that there are six elements of strategy for President Obama to consider:

1. Frame second-term policies from a more strategic and long-term perspective, recognizing the magnitude of the moment and the likelihood that the United States' actions now will have generational consequences.
2. Continue to emphasize what has been called "nation-building at home" as the first foreign policy priority, without neglecting its global context.
3. Recognize that the United States must energetically act to shape dynamic, uncertain global trends, or they will shape it unfavorably.
4. The United States must pursue more collaborative forms of leadership through deepening current alliances and interacting more effectively with a diverse set of actors to meet the challenges and opportunities of the dramatically changing times.
5. U.S. strategy to 2030 must deepen cooperation with China as the

most crucial single factor that will shape the international system in 2030.

6. U.S. leaders must more creatively address the focus of instability in the 21st century - the greater Middle East from North Africa to Pakistan - a major threat to U.S. strategy and world order.

The report is a good initiative to streamline policies and safeguard United States interests but, proverbially, 'humans see what they want to see' and 'perception is stronger than reality'. What this means is, we can present the case to the whole world in terms of whatever we want them to see because we have the media under our control. What really needs to be understood is, that events today move with much more rapidity than the pace of movement in the previous century - social media has certainly reshaped the whole media landscape - and, despite every effort being made to assert control over it, in the traditional sense the media is no longer in *their* hands.

One thing that is very clear from this report is that U.S. think tanks have admitted that soon there will be a "Post-Western World", and this could mean that the West is in trouble, with power sliding from West to East. Discussions on this hot topic are already underway in almost every major Western university; and another question under discussion is: what is the single most danger the world will face in the coming years? The answer to this question comes in just a single word "Protectionism". It seems inconceivable that the U.S., or for that matter Western think tanks, are completely ignoring the fast approaching and persistent danger of "Protectionism". Signs have already started to emerge as a result of the self-created and so-called "Recession". For some reason the media is not discussing this issue - either because they do not want to, or more likely, because they are being restrained; but the question is by whom?

One thing we can all agree is that this recession has created joblessness and this has ignited the emotive slogan "Protect the right of our own workers first". This will eventually create rifts between nation states and will put an end to globalization, which was pursued extensively throughout the previous three decades almost for the sole reason of making money. By creating this recession the West has instigated the policy of putting a stop to China's production. This has inevitably done some damage to the Chinese economy because

China's export figures have dropped. However, one thing needs to be understood - China has huge consumption within and around, so it can slow the growth levels but cannot put the full stop. If the recession should continue for more years to come then things will become out of control, as a result of damage to the core infrastructure within the U.S. and the European Union. There could be serious imbalance in the resources of East and West - as the aforementioned report states, wealth is shifting from West to East. The second element in the report caters for this particular aspect where emphasis is on "nation building at home", because there is already a realization that this recession has done enough damage.

Over the years there has been a built-up of a negative perception of America and now even if the U.S. behaves in a positive manner it is still viewed negatively. Afghanistan is a cockpit of Asia and to control central and south Asia it is very important that this strategically as well as tactically important country be controlled - but not through use of force, instead by installing real democracy. The present setup in Afghanistan hardly controls Kabul. A number of times the 'green zone'[58] within Kabul has been breached and things are still hostile inside the capital in spite of the presence of the most modern foreign troops in thousands. This is so far the longest war in the history of the U.S. and still Washington has not understood the prime lesson – that, the strategy they are following is not working. Yes, if their aim is to protect the image and reputation of the U.S. and leave Afghanistan forever then it is perfectly fine; but it is common knowledge that the U.S. wants to establish military bases in the country. Now the further question arises – will it be possible for those troops to stay back when whole the country returns to lawlessness, as apparently seems to be the case.

Nothing has been learned from the history of Afghanistan. The British have some idea, but does America give a damn about British

---

[58] colloquially referred to as the 'green zone' - ISAF was initially charged with securing Kabul and surrounding areas from the Taliban, al Qaeda and factional warlords, so as to allow for the establishment of the Afghan Transitional Administration headed by Hamid Karzai.

policies on Afghanistan? The most stable era in the Federal Administered Tribal Areas (FATA) is considered to be the one when the British Empire was ruling and the Frontier Crime Regulation (FCR) was put in place. The British ruled the area through local tribal elders and by doing so it was very well controlled. The FCR was specifically devised to counter any opposition from the Pashtuns (the tribe of Taliban) to British rule - their main objective was to protect the interests of the British Empire. More than a century has elapsed and these laws continue to be applied to FATA residents by the Government of Pakistan.

If we once again consider the geography of Afghanistan - it has total of 5,529km border, which includes 76km with China, 936km with Iran, 2430km with Pakistan, 1206km with Tajikistan, 744km with Turkmenistan, and 137km Uzbekistan. The four major ethnic groups in Afghanistan are Pashtun, Tajik, Hazara and Uzbek. Pashtun make up more than 50 per cent and are traditionally the rulers of Afghanistan. Tajik are almost 20 per cent of the total population, Hazara are almost 1.5 to 3 million in number and Uzbek are believed to be approximately 2 million, the remainder is made up of small minority ethnic groups. Now you can do your own sums out of the total population of Afghanistan, which is almost 31 million including 2.7 million refugees currently residing in Pakistan and Iran. The Taliban belong to the main ethnic group the Pashtun who have a population of almost 16 million, so practically speaking more than half the country is fighting directly or indirectly against the government (foreign troops) because any one not fighting has an affiliation with the tribe and disloyalty or dishonesty with the tribe is punishable by death according to Pashtun tradition.

One more factor needs clarification - from where does the role of India come into play? India claims to be the major player and has been observed running around dozen of Consulates in war torn Afghanistan. Who has given this role to India, and is it doing any good to this conflict or creating even more problems? Some commentators say India is flexing its muscles being a regional power; yet others say they are here to counter Pakistan's influence in Afghanistan; and one group says it is all about acquiring the natural resources within Afghanistan. Interestingly and in spite of huge U.S.

presence in the country Chinese companies are securing contracts in Afghanistan.

China's involvement in Afghanistan began with the investments made by Chinese firms to extract vast mineral wealth from Afghanistan, which is valued at about $1 trillion by the United States Geological Survey and $3 trillion by Afghanistan's Minister of Mines. In 2007 Metallurgical Corporation of China (MCC) and Jiangxi Copper Corporation Limited (JCCL) agreed to make the single largest foreign investment in Afghanistan to date, some $4.4 billion, when they won a tender to develop what geologists believe is the world's second largest undeveloped copper deposit at Aynak in Logar Province, 35km south-east of Kabul. In 2011 the China National Petroleum Corporation (CNPC) and its Afghan partner Watan Oil & Gas secured the rights to three oil blocks in the provinces of Sari-i-Pul and Faryab in north-western Afghanistan, in which CNPC expects to invest $400 million in its initial development.

The Islamic Republic of Iran[59] also has a role in present day Afghanistan and considers the U.S. presence in Afghanistan a major security concern along its 936km eastern border. It was deeply suspicious of the 2010 U.S. surge to dislodge Taliban forces from southern Afghanistan. Now Iranian leaders are more concerned about a left over U.S. presence after their withdrawal in 2014. On 11 January 2013 President Hamid Karzai visited the White House and announced that coalition forces will transition to a support role this spring. Tehran is keeping a close eye on the Bilateral Security Agreement under negotiation between Kabul and Washington, and actively trying to influence that debate inside Afghanistan as well as at the regional level.

---

[59] Iran – (Persian: ایران) also known as Persia. Officially the Islamic Republic of Iran since 1980 is a country in Western Asia. The country is bordered on the north by Armenia, Azerbaijan and Turkmenistan, with Kazakhstan and Russia to the north across the Caspian Sea. Iran is bordered on the east by Afghanistan and Pakistan, on the south by the Persian Gulf and the Gulf of Oman, on the west by Iraq and on the northwest by Turkey.

The five main drivers of current Afghan-Iranian relations are: narcotics, refugees, cultural and religious influence, water sharing, and last but not the least trade, investment and currency. As far as water sharing is concerned Afghanistan and Iran have a full treaty on the Helmand River water rights dating back to 1973, though there are tensions about the lack of verification and enforcement of the flow of water into Iran. The Kamal Khan Dam, which regulates the flow of water to Iran's Sistan Baluchistan Province, is a source of bitterness on both sides. On Cultural and religious influence peddling, there is increasing unease in Afghan political and cultural communities about unregulated Iranian funding of cultural, media and religious activities in Afghanistan, mainly to the Shiite Hazara, an ethnic minority. The Taliban systematically killed and displaced thousands of Hazara before 2001. Over the last decade Iranian relief organizations and businesses have reportedly funded construction of houses, libraries, roads, schools and clinics in several Afghan provinces, including Herat. While both countries are in favor of expanded economic and business ties, though the Afghan economy's weak base has mostly benefited surrounding countries, including Iran who has flooded Afghan markets with low-quality goods. The trade imbalance is further compounded by heavy Iranian investment in western Afghanistan. Iran has also destabilized Afghan markets by purchasing large amounts of foreign currency, a counter-measure against international sanctions on its nuclear program.

Iran's vision for Afghanistan and its own role is in flux and now tied to other factors such as: the nuclear standoff with the U.S. and Israel; the Saudi Arabian and changing Arab dynamics; the U.S. presence post-2014 where America wants to keep permanent bases; regional alignments and rivalries; and the state of its own economy and domestic political stability. Firstly, Iran prefers not to have to be concerned about Afghanistan, focusing on carving its own sphere of influence, accelerating a Western withdrawal, and assuring that its own interests are protected. Secondly, Iran is not in favor of a Western-influenced democratic, affluent Afghanistan; but at the same time is concerned that an unstable, opium producing and radicalized Afghanistan can also pose a major threat to its own interests, as experienced in the 1990s. Swayed between these two conflicting scenarios, and taking into consideration all other factors, Iran will try to prioritize its strategic and security needs in order to influence the course of events to the best of its abilities and given the resources at its disposal.

Possibly the course to any meaningful Indian role in Afghanistan is association with Iran. Iran alone can provide India with access for trade or provision of military support. To that extent it is important for India to understand the Iranian point of view and their thinking on the most important subject of Afghanistan. Iran has traditionally been hostile to the Taliban, and the return of the Taliban in power in Kabul cannot be viewed favorably by Iran. However in a given scenario Iran unequivocally can either play a negative role by seeking to keep American and Western attention and resources tied down in Afghanistan, or play a positive role by facilitating reconciliation and reconstruction. A prolonged U.S. engagement in Afghanistan suits Iran tactically, even if it has to temporarily support the Taliban. However Iran can equally play a very positive role in the reconstruction and pacification of Afghanistan provided it is permitted to do so. It can play the Tajik card and it may need help in doing so - an excellent support or use of the Iranian position that begs to be studied in more depth. Indeed there may be a need for steps by the West to diplomatically engage with Iran and reduce hostility with that State – but there are no signs of this happening in the near future as U.S. policy is changing toward Iran and this means Israeli's are not very happy.

Another story coming out of Afghanistan alludes to the present general dissatisfaction of the high level of corruption within the current regime, together with its inability to function in terms of limiting the role of NATO forces. NATO had pledged to restore peace and stability in Afghanistan and yet the continuing violence within the country, which has claimed the lives of thousands of civilians, somewhat reflects the past and could ultimately repeat the same old scenario by returning of Taliban to power.

Equally important, and what could in time prove responsible for the likely emergence of the Taliban in Afghanistan, are the recent differences between the Afghan president and high level U.S. officials.

On the one hand America is cynical about the role of President Karzai in Afghanistan; then on the other hand the Afghan president is criticizing America's role in the country saying that the U.S. is an occupying force pursuing its own national interest. It appears that developments so far have led the U.S. to act independently without involving President Karzai in said 'peace talks' with the Taliban. Although in the beginning both President Karzai's government and U.S. officials had been involved in negotiations with the Taliban, with view to the latter breaking ties with Al Qaeda and moving forward with peaceful purposes; but the most recent scenario indicates that the U.S. is involved unilaterally. Karzai himself shed light on the matter. In his recent public confirmation the Afghan president disclosed that the U.S. is holding direct talks with the Taliban - a development that the U.S. so far has not publicly acknowledged.

The main question arises here. If America feels it has to talk peace with the Taliban now (at the end) then why have they wasted so much time, money and the loss of so many lives, and subjected themselves to such embarrassment? Had America invested their resources and spent money investing in their up gradation of mindset visa vie Afghanistan then they really could have won the hearts and minds of the Afghan people a long time ago; now twelve years is a long time to change the opinion of the people. That said, talking is of course an excellent idea and the U.S. must indeed pursue this course of action openly, because if they truly desire peace after withdrawal then this is surely the only valid solution. If the correct foundation strategy is laid down for Afghanistan the country could still be controlled wisely by the U.S. without any further conflict.

This subject being of prime interest to me I am always willing to carry out further in-depth study regarding how we can bring peace and stability in the region by laying the correct strategy based on moral as well as ethical values. I have long believed that an ethical approach to conflict resolution will always bring lasting peace and stability. Without trying to preach, we more often forget the basic principals in the heat of the battle or our vision is so overblown that we do not care for the basics. I am sure those people who are at the helm of affairs and trying to resolve the Afghanistan conflict are considering all possible suggestions, but still I would like to make a few suggestions in a humble capacity. As far as I am aware there are a few fundamental principals of any conflict resolution.

First on the list is 'listen actively and carefully'. If we do not hear what other parties are communicating we cannot resolve a conflict. If we have pre-conceived ideas and we come with a preset mind or even preset agenda then resolution fails at the very first step. Is the U.S./NATO listening to everything that each of the major players has to say on Afghanistan; or do they force their way on preset policy in a top down approach? Are facts from history supporting the arguments being made, or being ignored and sending talks the other way around?

The second most important principal in any conflict resolution situation is to 'think before you react'. I believe things have been done in the past without observing the proper thinking process, and in so doing have damaged relationships. It takes a long time to make a relationship but only seconds to break that relationship. For instance, Pakistan is recognized as a major player in terms of the Afghanistan issue, there can be no doubt about it. The ground dictates clearly that via Pakistan these so called Mujahedeen's with the help of the U.S. defeated the former USSR, which was considered to be the most powerful land army. Lessons from the last twelve years tell us the fact - this wild horse (the Taliban) needs to be controlled by wisdom and not by force.

The third principal is to 'attack the problem not each other'. What is happening on the ground is that instead of stopping terrorism we are cultivating it. I would like to give the example of drone attacks. More than 90% of the Pakistani population, including the government of Pakistan, hates the use of U.S. drone attacks within Pakistan after violating sovereign borders of the country. Although, under pressure, the government agrees to the demands of U.S. covertly, again up to 90% of the casualties are civilians and these include women and children who are dying. On a number of occasions the Afghan President has openly criticized U.S./NATO over such attacks where civilian casualties have occurred. You can imagine the Afghan President must be under extreme pressure but even then he has taken this direct confrontation route with the U.S. by declaring it openly on the media. Keep in mind that he is known to be the man of the West. The famous British journalist Christina Lamb wrote in one of her articles in 2009, "When Hamid Karzai is re-inaugurated as President today after one of the world's dodgiest elections, everyone from Washington to Whitehall will be watching for some sign that he will clean up his act. If he doesn't, many - including U.S. Ambassador Karl Eikenberry - believe it will be well nigh impossible to defeat the Taliban, however many troops President Obama might ultimately decide to send." Her article continued, "Britain's Prime Minister Gordon Brown has described the Karzai government as a 'byword for corruption' and warned he will 'forfeit' international support if he doesn't improve." The Obama administration has given the same message and suggested a list of clean names they would like to see in the cabinet. She describes how Karzai became President of Afghanistan, in her words, "I was in Herat when he was named interim President after the fall of the Taliban, and most Afghans I met had never heard of him. In fact, the hastily convened Bonn conference of Afghan representatives to choose an interim leader did not vote for him; their choice was Abdul Sattar Seerat, a former justice minister close to the ex-king. But the international community feared he would not be acceptable, as he did not come from the majority Pashtun tribe. Karzai had won just three votes". I have quoted these references because if such a President speaks out against the West then things must be pretty serious and he is clearly under extreme pressure on both sides.

Coming back to the third principle, terrorism is the common enemy so the aim should be to eliminate that, and not instead to start targeting each other. Remember Pakistan is the biggest victim in this conflict in terms of human life, in terms of infrastructure, in terms of economic growth. It is the only country in the world where terrorism has taken the lives of people on all levels from common citizens, serving soldiers, on up to an army General, and a serving minister. The total death toll is nearly 50,000 human lives.

Coming on to next simple principle 'accept responsibility'. When you start to place the blame it creates resentment and anger. Mostly blaming will increase when you fail in achieving your goal then you start to look for scapegoats. This does not help because it can make the situation even worse. This is exactly what is going on in

Afghanistan where the Afghan government is blaming foreign troops and its neighbours. U.S. led forces are blaming corruption within the government, neighbouring interference, etc. Mistakes have to be accepted before they can be corrected. Only when you admit and confess that your policy or strategy was or is wrong, then can you implement corrective measures.

The next principle is use of 'direct communication' because this can solve things quicker. If messages are clear and non-threatening, the assimilation process is better, and this can lead to positive results. If all parties can look for common interest/ground this is far better than trying to sort out their own interests without giving due consideration and importance to the interests of the other major players which can lead to complications. It is understandable that each player will have their own agenda but, at the same time as safeguarding their own interests, if they also cater for the interests of others this can more often than not bring fruitful and quicker results.

Last but not the least 'focus on the future of relationship' if you are honest in your approach. Michael Arnold, Australian Army Brigadier, whose civilian occupation is lecturer at Deakin University where he lectures in strategy, security and international relations, is currently undertaking a Doctorate of Philosophy at Deakin University. His thesis relates to Australian defence policy. He explains the criteria for successful interventions in his article 'Intervention', which he has contributed to a book Contemporary Security and Strategy. He explains these seven points for successful interventions.

1. Just cause and political legitimacy: needed for international community support.
2. All other avenues to resolve conflict exhausted: this included diplomacy, economic sanctions and threat for the use of force.
3. Viability and reasonable chance that will improve circumstances: this effectively rules out action against large, strong states or states with WMD. Will an intervention trigger a protracted insurgency or draw in a powerful neighbour or trigger a worse conflict?
4. Strong, unwavering political resolve.
5. Clear political aim and unequivocal mission for the military commander: a strong and robust mandate is essential for success and mission creep must be avoided.

6. Unity of command and core force competence.
7. Appropriate force balance and size.

I would not like to comment on these criteria because the points are quite self-explanatory and one can easily judge if Afghan intervention was successful or not. Our aim now should be to sort out this complex scenario and do the right thing, because, if we are wrong again then history will repeat itself and the price could be even higher.

Steve Brooking, Head of Analysis and Policy Unit, United Nations Assistance Mission in Afghanistan (UNAMA) in his brief paper published under the title Coordinating The International Community, writes and I quote: "Indeed one of the problems with Afghanistan from 2001-2012 has been that, because of competing agendas, there has been no overall co-ordination attempted or allowed, and - with the exception of brief period during the initial military campaign - no real 'leadership' by an authorized powerful body that could attempt such co-ordination."

Lt Gen (Retd) Professor Sir Paul Newton KBE, who is currently Director of the newly created Strategy and Security Institute, University of Exeter, UK, is known to be one of the most distinguished armed forces officers with unmatchable experience and expertise. In 2003 he became the Chief of Defence Staff's Liaison Officer to the Chairman of the US Joint Chiefs in Washington, working on Iraq. Deploying to Baghdad as the Deputy, Strategic Planning in HQ Multi-National Force Iraq, he was awarded the US Legion of Merit. In January 2005 he took over the PJHQ Intelligence Division. Promoted to Major General in February 2006, he briefly returned to the Royal College of Defence Studies as Army Director before returning to Baghdad to lead the Coalition reconciliation effort heading a new Force Strategic Engagement Cell, for which he was awarded a Legion of Merit, First Oak Leaf Cluster. He later ran the MOD Development, Concepts and Doctrine Centre producing Global Strategic Trends, the first UK doctrine for stabilisation and the MOD position paper on the Future Character of Conflict, in time for the Security and Defence Review. In April 2010 Lieutenant General Newton became Commander Force Development &

Training and a member of the Executive Committee of the Army Board, charged with 'leading and driving' change.

He writes in his article titled 'Intervention and state building' and I quote: "More worrying is that inter-agency ways of working have not been locked into post-Afghan structures, much less cultures. Unless institutionalized now, they will not be available in future crises where humanitarian need, risk and vital interests intersect. Whether deployed under a 'state building' banner or less contentious mandate, or a combination of the two given that most conflicts evolve incrementally, closer integration of all the levers of power is essential given the prevalence of fragile states, growing populations and urbanization. In Afghanistan, the international community's assumptions about Taliban resilience, and thus the scale and pace of effort, were plain wrong, thus in part setting the conditions for a protracted 'stabilization' mission. It is one in which the military continues to play a disproportionate role, for example, leading anti-corruption efforts." The conflict in Afghanistan has local dimensions that have harmed that people alongside global dimensions that are well known. History has shown that neglect of Afghanistan and its problems could eventually damage the entire region. The discontinuation of war there may lead to stability in the whole region, while the continuation of the war will be a scourge that affects many. Therefore, all parties are responsible for finding a solution to the problem and helping people get out of the current crisis.

There is no doubt that the Afghan issue is a thorny and complicated one due to the opposing and contradictory positions of the internal parties involved. This includes the current government, peaceful opposition parties, the Taliban, the Hezb Islami led by Hekmatyar, and neighbouring countries like Iran and Pakistan who are also looking after their own interests. These two states have an influence on Afghan authorities and each has its own mechanisms and ways to influence the course of reconciliation in Afghanistan.

The Taliban have two major points of contention. That firstly, talks should be held through a formal office in which they have diplomatic representation. The Taliban rejects all of the talks between the government and its members to date, as it believes the purpose of these talks is to deliver its members to the government rather than settling the Afghan issue. Secondly, the Taliban believes that talks cannot be for the purpose of joining the current system of government but should be to form a new political system through the development of a new constitution for the country. It justifies its rejection of the current constitution by saying that it was written under American pressure.

The Afghan government is in a dilemma because the Taliban refuses to engage in any dialogue with it until foreign troops withdraw from the country. The government has also been excluded from the occasional secret talks between the United States and the Taliban in a number of European and Arab countries. The President, therefore, fears the marginalisation of the government's role in resolving the issue.

In light of above analysis and the positions of the influential parties in the Afghan issue, it can be said that talks between the United States and the Taliban in their current format will not produce tangible or meaningful results because of the blatant contrast between their interests and the two parties opposing purposes in the peace talks. One of the parties will have to compromise some of its basic principles, which is unlikely in the current circumstances. The United States does not seem inclined to compromise its objectives and is not ready to withdraw all of its troops because they believe that this would amount to a security threat. If that happens, the last thirteen years will have been in vain. In addition, the new generation of the Taliban do not want to approve of the existence of US bases in Afghanistan because that would forfeit their purpose and everything they have fought for.

The positions of the different Afghan parties are not as contradictory and distant; they can overcome their problems and bring their views closer together through serious talks if they sincerely intend on doing so. Here I am not referring to the Afghan government and the Taliban but rather the various Afghan parties including those that are part of the government, the armed opposition and the political opposition. If compatibility were achieved between all Afghan parties to determine the features of the next system of government, it would be easier to expel foreign troops. Hence, it is suggested / recommended that simultaneous dialogue is initiated

between the different Afghan parties and between the Taliban and the United States. For the talks to succeed in resolving the Afghan issue, they must take into consideration the following matters:
- Neutral Afghan parties must mediate between the various Afghan parties; they must have the confidence of all the parties involved. The High Peace Council was not successful because the Taliban considers it is a government body and therefore unable to maintain neutrality in talks.
- Within the framework of the Council of Islamic Cooperation, an axis of strong Islamic countries must embrace and support the peace talks in Afghanistan. This will enable decisions to be implemented and persuade western countries, especially the United States, to accept the outcomes of the talks and assist in building state institutions after stabilisation. The countries that make up the axis cannot have ambitions in Afghanistan or influence their neighbours, especially Pakistan. These countries include Saudi Arabia, Egypt, Iran, Pakistan, Turkey, Malaysia and Qatar.
- An office with Afghan experts and academic specialists should be established in Kabul with the assistance of experts from outside Afghanistan to advise entities that seek reconciliation.
- The initial focus must be on restoring mutual confidence between the warring Afghan parties, first, through multiple meetings and, second, through concrete steps that indicate that the parties are serious about the reconciliation process and that it is not just a fake trap.
- Various Afghan parties should be brought to the dialogue table to agree on a plan for reaching stability in Afghanistan.
- The Afghan people should be encouraged to support those seeking reconciliation between the various parties.

Promote Economic Development

Afghanistan is one of the world's poorest countries, and endemic poverty has made some elements of the population susceptible to Taliban overtures. Moreover, failed and deprived states frequently become incubators for terrorism, drug and human trafficking, and other illicit activities. Therefore, efforts at reconciliation should be coupled with a broad internationally led effort to promote economic

development. Potentially useful measures include:
- Giving Afghanistan preferential trading status with the U.S., Europe, Japan and other leading global economies.
- Promoting investment in local and national infrastructure by national and international companies.
- Providing subsidies, loans, and technical assistance to local (non-poppy) agricultural producers, construction companies, and artisans.
- Promoting "special reconstruction zones" for foreign and domestic companies to produce export goods. Such zones could offer investors preferential tax treatment and access to enhanced security and infrastructure measures, at least initially.
- Helping Afghan women directly through micro-lending and educational support programs, and by making some portion of U.S. assistance conditional on the protection of basic human rights, especially women's rights.
- Considering the purchase of Afghanistan's poppy crop, to give Afghan farmers immediate economic gains, reduce Taliban revenues, and reduce the flow of illicit narcotics to the West.

To the extent possible, external assistance should be channelled through a more decentralized Afghan government. Such decentralization would build capacity, give legitimacy to the government itself, enhance transparency, and limit corruption. Decentralization ensures that aid monies go directly to helping Afghans rather than to consultants, NGOs, and other international agencies.

Involve Global and Regional Stakeholders

The Afghanistan conflict reflects long-standing rivalries among the different ethnic and tribal groups within the country, but it has long been exacerbated by outside powers seeking to protect or advance their own interests.

The United States now bears a growing share of the costs of this conflict, even though virtually all of Afghanistan's neighbours have larger and more immediate stakes in its resolution. Despite their considerable differences, neighbouring states such as India, Pakistan, China, and Iran share a common interest in preventing Afghanistan from either being dominated by any single power or remaining a failed state that exports instability.

The U.S. military role should be eliminated and converted into a UNO role with an energetic diplomatic effort, spearheaded by the United Nations and strongly backed by the United States and its allies. I think the United Kingdom can play a big part here, having been fully involved in the conflict and having a better understanding of this issue. The UK also enjoys good relations with Pakistan. This initiative should seek a formal commitment to Afghan neutrality and a resolution of existing border disputes. They need agreements to recognize and support the more inclusive and decentralized Afghan government. The United States should also use its influence to reduce tensions among the various regional actors - especially between India and Pakistan - in order to decrease their tendency to see Afghanistan as an arena for conflict or to view the Taliban or other non-state groups as long-term strategic assets.

The United States should also place greater reliance on allies and partners whose ability to work with Afghans exceeds our own. Non-Arab Muslim states such as Indonesia and Turkey - the latter a NATO ally - if present on the ground, could play substantial mentoring roles in the areas of education, political reform, and human rights. Such states could help Afghanistan conform to international standards as well as their own principles.

Abandoning a predominantly military focus could actually facilitate a more spirited diplomatic effort. As long as the U.S. military is doing the heavy lifting against the Taliban, the Afghan government has no immediate need to broaden its base. Other states can free ride on the U.S. effort, and regional actors can pursue their own agendas at less risk. Once the U.S. signals that its patience is not infinite and that its military campaign is over, then contenders for power within Afghanistan and its neighbours will have a greater incentive to negotiate agreements designed to stabilize the situation. Most importantly, Pakistan should be taken seriously, accepted as a main player and included in all talks, because without their involvement this complex issue cannot be solved. I am not wrong when I state that future settlement in Afghanistan is not in the hands of the U.S.A but in the hands of Pakistan and Afghanistan.

With the Afghanistan Surge, the U.S. has been spending almost $100 billion per year in Afghanistan, with a stated primary purpose of eradicating just 20 to 30 Al Qaeda leaders, and in a country whose total GDP is only $14 billion per annum. This is a serious imbalance of expenses to benefit. $100 billion per year is more than the entire annual cost of the Obama administration's new health care plan and is money that could be used to better counter global terrorist threats, reduce the $1.7 trillion annual deficit, repair and modernize a large portion of U.S. infrastructure, radically enhance American educational investment, launch a massive new Manhattan Project-like effort on energy alternatives research, or be used for other critical purposes.

The U.S. military budget has grown from $370 billion in 2000 to $707 billion in 2011, and this current Middle East conflict is now the second most expensive war in U.S. history, behind only World War II. This war is more expensive than the Vietnam and Korean Wars combined. It is now the longest war in U.S. history.

The United States should not by any means think that have or will abandon Afghanistan, but it is time to abandon the current strategy that is not working. Trying to pacify Afghanistan by force of arms will not work. A costly military campaign like this is more likely to jeopardize America's vital security interests than to protect them. I believe that the United States should pursue more modest goals that are both consistent with America's true interests and far more likely to succeed.

Chapter 13

Conclusion

As per my understanding the United States has only two vital interests in the Afghanistan-Pakistan (Afghan-Pak) region:
1. Preventing Afghanistan from being a "safe haven" from which Al Qaeda or other extremists can organize more effective attacks on the U.S. homeland; and
2. Ensuring that Pakistan's nuclear arsenal does not fall into hostile hands.

Protecting U.S. interests does not require a U.S. military victory over the Taliban. A Taliban takeover is unlikely even if the United States reduces its military commitment. The Taliban is a rural insurgency rooted primarily in Afghanistan's Pashtun population, and succeeded due in some part to the disenfranchisement of rural Pashtuns. The Taliban's seizure of power in the 1990s was due to an unusual set of circumstances that no longer exists and are unlikely to be repeated if tackled properly, with close cooperation with Pakistan, as the Taliban logistically rely on Pakistan and are already divided in various factions.

There is no momentous Al Qaeda present in Afghanistan today, and the risk of a new 'safe haven' there under more 'friendly' Taliban rule is quite overstated. Should an Al Qaeda chamber regroup in Afghanistan, the UNO and not the USA should have residual military capability in the region sufficient to track and destroy.

The world needs to understand that Pakistan is facing a serious propaganda problem for obvious reasons. Despite its cooperative and transparent foreign and strategic policies, many international security observers express their unjustifiable anxiety about the country's nuclear program in particular and the armed forces in general. Recently, once again, a taskforce of security analysts repeated their concocted concerns regarding Pakistan's nuclear program following the aftermath of the Peshawar School shooting incident.

Pakistan is an atomic state and has a very powerful army which I surely think is quite capable of looking after country's nuclear arsenal, therefore preaching rumours or slogans like "rouge state" and not capable of looking after its arsenals seems just a mere propaganda. Such reports/rumours are mostly Indian oriented and their only aim is to create bad image of Pakistan, which International community must understand.

Pakistan's fragile new government led by Mr Nawaz Sharif could be confronting a nuclear related pressure in the near future. The United States controlled Western nations have already been pressurizing Islamabad to enter into the Fissile Material Cut-off Treaty negotiations at the Conference on Disarmament. Ironically, what they want from Pakistan is to sacrifice its option to produce weapon grade fissile material without considering its proposal to negotiate, constitute and finally implement a treaty, which would not only prohibit the current production of fissile material, but also ensure the elimination of the existing weapon-grade fissile material. Pakistani think tanks have already predicted that Pakistanis should be vigilant about the new wave of nuclear discourse in international media. Maybe, the subjects and arguments will be the same, but the actors could be different.

Afghanistan provides many examples of the wisdom of Winston Churchill saying, "those that fail to learn from history are doomed to repeat it". Great Britain forgot the hard-learned lessons from the first Anglo Afghan War (1839-42) and got caught in the misadventure of the second Anglo Afghan War (1878-80). The Afghan Communist government that took power in a military coup in 1978 did not appear to have learned from the failed westernization and reform experiment of King Amanullah (1919-29). It imposed radical changes and engaged in brutal repression, quickly stirring up a violent reaction that threatened the new regime. The Soviet Union enthusiastically viewed its military intervention in Afghanistan at the end of 1979 as a limited action with short time horizon assumptions that prove woefully unfounded and whose lack of realism would have been apparent from a review of Afghan history. Likewise it is not apparent that the United States and its NATO allies learned any lessons from the Soviet occupation when they initiated their joint military intervention in Afghanistan after 9/11.

The possibility of Afghanistan's neighbours playing 'spoiler' roles and the regional rivalries undermining transition and beyond is very real. Historical experience and the current situation in Pakistan indicate that there is a need to plan around, or at a minimum for contingency planning, with respect to Pakistan for example preventing a meaningful peace agreement with the Taliban factions otherwise real peace is in danger.

The post-Soviet withdrawal period indicates the potential and limitations of Afghan security forces. Holding onto Kabul and other large cities is probably the most we can hope for. Indeed, more risks may be associated with the Afghan National Army (ANA) during and after the current transition given greater ethnic factionalization; parts of the ANA could fragment or desert earlier rather than later. There are already such incidents being reported where police and army personnel have deserted and joined Taliban factions.

Effective Afghan leadership and following a national agenda is very critical for achieving positive outcomes in times of change and transition in Afghanistan, including complete foreign military withdrawals. International experience also stresses the importance of effective national leadership during transitions, as emphasized in the 2011 World Development Report Conflict, Security, and Development. The present power transition formula by the USA seems fragile.

Afghanistan's challenging experience over the past four decades with divisive, ideologically and ethnically driven political parties has made political parties in general a curse to many Afghans, but effective political parties are an essential ingredient in successful democracies around the world, and the post-2001 period has seen that more nationally oriented political parties have not emerged and developed. This important aspect should have been taken care of but unfortunately there are no solid measures in place to create a strong national party consisting of leaders from all the ethnic backgrounds accepted by the Afghan people.

While giving answers to the most important question of why we could not win the war in Afghanistan Mr Jack Fairweather, currently a fellow of the Centre for Middle Eastern Studies, Harvard University; also the *Daily Telegraph's* Baghdad and Gulf correspondent for five years, and an expert on the American and British military campaigns in Iraq and Afghanistan, and author of 'A War of Choice: Britain in Iraq 2003-9', and also, 'The Good War: Why We Couldn't Win the War or the Peace in Afghanistan', said and I quote:

"There was a fundamental mistake that was made in conflating the threat posed by al-Qaida with that of the Taliban. Al-Qaida was this international jihadist group that had already killed thousands of Americans. The Taliban was a much more local, tribal-based organization that ran a repressive regime in Afghanistan. You may remember that famous speech by Bush on September 20, 2001, where he said you're either with us or against us. In setting up the rhetoric for what became the War on Terror, he lumped together al-Qaida and the Taliban. The U.S. military got rid of al-Qaida from Afghanistan pretty quickly, but then they started fighting and targeting, arresting, detaining, Taliban fighters. I think one of the great mistakes of the war, that's not fully appreciated, was the way in which Taliban commanders who were ready to lay down their arms were riled up by U.S. actions."

While talking about Afghanistan's future he says, "I think those who knew Afghanistan in 2001, and visit the capital now, Kabul, are amazed by the transformations that have taken place... There's a change. I always think back to a trip I made to Afghanistan in 2012 when I went out to an outpost in Helmand with the U.S. military to an Afghanistan police checkpoint and the radio, the police radio, was on and the Afghanistan police officer was having a conversation with his Taliban opposite number about 400 yards away. And they were exchanging insults at first, but then as the sun began to set they began singing songs to each other, and before you knew it they were talking about their girlfriends, talking about their teenage hopes and dreams. If the West can help that police officer and that Taliban teenager find common ground, that's where the future lies."

The bottom line is if USA along with NATO could not succeed in Afghanistan with all its mighty power and billions of dollars spent and practically lost the longest war in American history then the question arises can this conflict be solved by a blame game? The answer to this question is "NO". We have to learn from our mistakes and should try listening to what people like Christina Lamb, OBE, and one of Britain's leading foreign correspondents, has to say. She has been named Foreign Correspondent of the Year five times in the British Press Awards and What The Papers Say Awards and in 2007 was winner of the Prix Bayeux Calvados, one of the worlds most prestigious prizes for war correspondents, for her reporting from Afghanistan. Christina is currently roving Foreign Affairs correspondent for the *Sunday Times*, and has been a foreign correspondent for more than twenty years, living in Pakistan, Brazil and South Africa first for the *Financial Times* then the *Sunday Times*.

In her new book entitled 'Farewell Kabul: How The West Ignored Pakistan and Lost Afghanistan', she tells how the west turned success into defeat in the longest war fought by the United State in its history and by Britain since the Hundred Years War. According to her it is the story of well-intentioned men and women going into a place they did not understand at all; and how what had once been the right thing to do had become a conflict that everyone wanted to exit. It has been a fiasco, which left Afghanistan still one of the poorest and most dangerous nations on earth. The current President of the United States Barak Obama's visit to India and totally ignoring Pakistan is a clear-cut signal that Pakistan will be ignored again. This time if we ignore and try to put blame on Pakistan only then the result will be no different. I hope this time well-intentioned men and women are not repeating the same mistake and going to a place, which they still do not understand at all.

When we will learn from our mistakes only God knows!

"There has never been a protracted war from which a country has benefited." - Sun Tzu

Some Interesting Facts about Afghanistan

1. The New Year in Afghanistan, called Nawroz, is celebrated on 21 March, which is the first day of spring.
2. The largest city in Afghanistan is Kabul, the capital.
3. Afghanistan is a landlocked country sharing borders with Iran, Pakistan, Uzbekistan, Turkmenistan, Tajikistan and China.
4. Poetry is a big part of Afghans' culture and it has been for centuries. In the city of Herat, women, men and children gather on Thursday night to share verses from old and new poetry.
5. The people of Afghanistan are called Afghans and not Afghanis, which is the currency - a most common mistake that happens.
6. The official language of Afghanistan is Dari and Pashto. They speak several other languages as well such as Persian, Uzbek and Turkmen to name a few.
7. Afghanistan's main source of income comes from agriculture. They produce large amounts of crops that are enough to provide for the people and export as well. They plant vegetables, fruits, rice and nuts.
8. Afghanistan is also rich in natural resources with the main ones being natural gas and oil.
9. Afghanistan's national game is called Buzkashi, or in other words, 'goat-grabbing'. It is a sport where the players in two teams on horseback try to grab a goat carcass and drag it toward a goal. It has been played for centuries (though banned by the Taliban) and it even attracts sponsors nowadays.
10. Afghanistan celebrates its independence from Britain on 19 August. Though Afghanistan was not actually part of the British Colonies, they went to war three times until Afghanistan declared its independence in 1919.
11. The main mountain range in Afghanistan is the Hundu Kush. It is a massive range with mountains at around 24,000 feet. 'Kush' comes from the verb 'kushtan' which means 'to kill' so Hindu Kush means 'Hindu Killer.' Mountaineering tourism has become very popular in recent years; Hindu killing is a thing of the past.

12. The Greeks built a Metropolis at Ai Khanoum in northern Afghanistan at around 400BC. It had a gymnasium, a theatre, had dedications in Greek to Hercules and Herakles and a huge statue to Zeus. The tomb of the founder of Ai Khanoum was inscribed:

"Païs ôn kosmios ginou (As children, learn good manners)
hèbôn enkratès, (as young men, learn to control the passions)
mesos dikaios (in middle age, be just)
presbutès euboulos (in old age, give good advice)
teleutôn alupos" (then die, without regret.)

Greek influence can be found all over Afghanistan, Pakistan and China.

About The Author

Imran Hanif spent 20 years in the Pakistan Army before retiring and moving to the United Kingdom. He graduated from the prestigious Pakistan Military Academy (PMA) as a commissioned officer in 1991. The PMA is equal to Sandhurst in United Kingdom and West Point in the USA. During his military service he held various staff and command appointments. He has been a GSO-2 (operations) at Brigade level CAF HQ and 2nd in Command of an Infantry Regiment. He commanded three different Wings of Civil Armed Forces (CAF) in interior Baluchistan, one on the Pak-Afghan border during the Taliban's regime. He is also a graduate of the Centre of Excellence in Stability Police Management (COESPU) from Italy. He took early retirement in 2008 at his own request to pursue his Post Graduation degree of Master of Business Administration (MBA) in the UK. He also completed a Post Graduate degree in Strategic Management and Leadership from the Chartered Management Institute (CMI) UK. He achieved the ultimate accolade in management and became a Chartered Manager (CMgr) and Fellow of the Chartered Management Institute (FCMI). He is also a member of the International Professional Security Association (IPSA) and keeps abreast of the latest developments in the field of security. He is a freelance trainer in the field of Conflict Management, Physical Intervention and Security Guarding within the Private Security Industry and Occupational Health & Safety. Nowadays he is pursuing his own business goals in the UK and working toward his PhD.

About Dr Zafar Nawaz Jaspal

Presently Dr Zafar Nawaz Jaspal is a director and Associate Professor at School of Politics and International Relations, Quaid-I Azam University, Islamabad. He holds a Ph.D. in International Relations. His Dissertation title was "South Asian Nuclearizaiton: Implications for Regional Security and Nuclear Non Proliferation Regime. He is a well-known distinguished scholar and a Published author with research articles published in various Journals all over the world. He has actively taken part in more than hundred conferences around the globe. Details of his work are as under:

Book
1. Nuclear Risk Reduction Measures and Restrain Regime in South Asia (New Delhi: Manohar, & Colombo: Regional Center for Strategic Studies, 2004)

Journals / Research Articles
2. "Nuclear/Radiological Terrorism: Myth or Reality," Journal of Political Studies, Vol.19, Issue, 1, Summer 2012, pp. 91-111. (HEC-Y)
3. "Evolution of Pakistan's Nuclear Program: Debates in its Decision-Making," Regional Studies, Vol.XXX, No. 2, Spring 2012, pp. 3-38. (HEC-Y)
4. "2012 Conference on Disarmament: Pakistan's Approach Towards lFMCT" Policy Perspective, Vol. 9. No. 2, 2012, pp. 17-32.
5. "A Comparative Analysis of the Policies of the EU and Pakistan on the Iranian Nuclear Issue," Journal of European Studies, Vol. 28, No. 1, January 2012, pp. 99-117. (HEC-Y)
6. "Towards Nuclear Zero in South Asia: Realistic Narrative." Irish Studies in International Affairs, Vol. 22, 2011, pp. 75-97 (Foreign-Ireland).
7. "Ballistic Missile Defense: Implications for India-Pakistan Strategic Environment," NDU Journal, Vol. XXV, 2011, pp. 1-26. (HEC-Z)

8. "Af-Pak and Regional Peace in China's Perspective: A Critical Appraisal," Pakistan Horizon, Vol. 64, No. 4, October, 2011, pp. 29-50. (HEC-Y)
9. "Threat of Extremism and Terrorist Syndicate Beyond FATA," Journal of Political Studies, Vol. 17, Issue 2, Winter 2010. pp. 19-49. (HEC-Y)
10. "Future of FMCT: Assessing the Prospects and Constraints," Strategic Studies, Vol. XXX, No. 1 & 2, Spring & Summer 2010, pp. 46-71. (HEC-Y)
11. "Paradox of Deterrence: India-Pakistan Strategic Relations" Strategic Studies, Vol. XXIX, No. 4, Winter 2009. (HEC-Y)
12. "War and Strategic Environment: Actors for Change and Future Wars," Margalla Papers, Winter 2009. (HEC-Z)
13. "WMD Terrorism and Pakistan: Counterterrorism," Defence Against Terrorism Review, Vol. 1, No. 2, Fall 2008. (Foreign-Turkey)
14. "Indo-US Nuclear Deal: Altering Global Nuclear Order," Strategic Studies, Vol: XXVII, Nos. 2 & 3 summer & autumn 2008. (HEC-Y)
15. "Pakistan and the issue of Nuclear Proliferation," Margalla Papers, Special Edition—Nuclear Pakistan: Ten Years On, 2008. (HEC-Z)
16. "Pakistan & Global War on Terrorism," Journal of Political Studies, Summer 2008. (HEC-Y)
17. "Indo-US Nuclear Deal: Endeavor to Surpass Restrains," Defence Journal, November 2007. (HEC-Y)
18. "Enhanced Defence Cooperation between the United States and Pakistan," Strategic Insights, Vol. VI, Issue 4, June 2007. (Foreign, United States)
19. "Pakistan's Judicial System: Curbing the menace of Terrorism," Pakistan Horizon, Vol. 60, No.1, January 2007. (HEC-Y)
20. "Indo-U.S. Nuclear Deal: Implication for Indo-Pak Peace Process," Margalla Papers, 2006. (HEC-Z)
21. "Confidence Building Measures: Proposals and Concrete Steps" Journal of Political Studies, Issue X, winter 2006. (HEC-Y)
22. "Nuclear Risk's Preventive Approaches in an Adversarial Indo-Pakistan Scenario," IPRI Journal, Vol. VI, No.1, winter 2006 (HEC-Y)
23. "Pakistan's nuclear Philosophy and Missile Potential," Defence Journal, November 2006. (HEC-Y)

24. "Nuclear Weapons Proliferation: Role of Pakistan?," Al- Siyasa A Journal of Politics, Society & Culture, Issue VIII, Winter 2005.
25. "Operation Iraqi Freedom & WMD: Implications for Global Politics," IPRI Journal, Vol. V, No.1, Winter 2005. (HEC-Y)
26. "Non-Proliferation Treaty Ambiguities," Defence Journal, January 2005. (HEC-Y)
27. "Nuclear Capable Navies of India and Pakistan: Impact on the Strategic Environment of the Indian Ocean," IPRI Journal, Vol. IV, No. 1, Winter 2004. (HEC-Y)
28. "Nuclear Weapons & Nuclear Terrorism", Defence Journal, November 2004. (HEC-Y)
29. "Pakistan Responsibility & Export Control Law 2004," Defence Journal, October 2004. (HEC-Y)
30. "Ghauri-1, BrahMos, Agni A-I missile Tests: Significance?" Defence Journal, August 2004. (HEC-Y)
31. India-Pakistan Nuclear CBMs" A Step in the Right Direction," Defence Journal, July 2004. (HEC-Y)
32. "Congress Victory: Implications for India-Pakistan Peace Process," Defence Journal, June 2004. (HEC-Y)
33. "Nuclear CBMs between India and Pakistan: Utilitarian Approach," Defence Journal, May 2004. (HEC-Y)
34. "Shaheen-11 test-fire, Reassuring Pakistan's Deterrence," Defence Journal, April 2004. (HEC-Y)
35. "Pakistan: A Responsible Nuclear Weapon State?," Defence Journal, March 2004. (HEC-Y)
36. "Pakistan's Defence Policy: Imperative and Rationale of Missile," Al- Siyasa A Journal of Politics, Society & Culture, Issue V, Summer 2003.
37. "India's Look East Policy: New Challenges for Pakistan," IPRI Journal, Vol. 2, No. 3, winter 2003. (HEC-Y)
38. "Emerging Trends in Terrorism", Al- Siyasa A Journal of Politics, Society & Culture, Issue 111, Fall 2002.
39. "Bush's Strategic Framework: Impact on Nuclear Non-Proliferation Regime" Pakistan Journal of American Studies, Vol. 20, No. 2, Fall 2002. (HEC-Z)
40. "Maligning Pakistan's nuclear programme: Old wine in a New Bottle," Defence Journal December 2002.

41. "India's Anti- Ballistic Missile Program: Impact on Pakistan's Security," IPRI Journal, Vol. 2, No. 2, summer 2002. (HEC-Y)
42. "National Security Council: Implications for Pakistan's Political System," Defence Journal, March 2002. (HEC-Y)
43. "Safety and Security of Pakistan's Nuclear Capabilities: A Critical Analysis," IPRI Journal, Vol.2, No. 1, winter 2002. (HEC-Y)
44. "FMCT: Policy Option for Pakistan," National Development and Security Vol. ix, No.4, Serial No. 36, summer 2001.
45. "India's Endorsement of the US BMD: Challenges for Regional Stability," IPRI Journal, Vol.1, No. 1, summer 2001. (HEC-Y)
46. "Afghanistan Crisis: A Pragmatic Approach," Defence Journal, November 2001. (HEC-Y)
47. "Missile Defence Systems: US-China relations," Defence Journal, August 2001. (HEC-Y)
48. "Reassessing Pakistan's Nuclear Strategy," Defence Journal, July 2001 (HEC-Y).
49. "India's Missiles Capabilities: Regional Implications," Pakistan Horizon, Vol. 54, No. 1, January 2001. (HEC-Y)
50. "US BMD: Leading to a New Era of Arms Race?," Strategic Studies, Vol. xxi, No.1, Spring 2001. (HEC-Y)
51. "NPT In 2000: Challenges Ahead," Strategic Studies, Vol. xx, No.4, Autumn 2000. (HEC-Y)
52. "A Case for Signing CTBT," Strategic Issues, No. 3, March 2000.
53. "CTBT: Salient Features and Implications for Pakistan", National Development and Security, Vol. VII, No. 4, Serial No.28, May 1999.
54. Tactical Nuclear Weapon: Deterrence Stability between Indian and Pakistan," in 2001- 2012 US-Pakistan Strategic Partnership: A Track II Dialogue, Centre on Contemporary Conflict, Naval Postgraduate School, Monterey. http://www.nps.edu/Academics/Centers/CCC/PASCC/Publications/2012/2012_002_Jaspal.pdf
55. "Strategic Response to Nuclear/Radiological Terrorist Attacks," in Dan-Radu Voica, Mustafa Kibaroglu, Response to Nuclear and Radiological Terrorism (Amsterdam, IOS Press: 2011), pp. 57-72.
56. "India's Ballistic Missile Defence System Development & Pakistan's Countermeasures: Catalyst for Deterrence Instability in South Asia," in Zulfqar Khan, ed. Nuclear Pakistan: Strategic Dimensions (Karachi: Oxford University Press, 2011), pp. 85-119.

57. "Nuclear Confidence Building Measures between India and Pakistan: Possible Alternatives" in Bhumitra Chakma," ed. Politics of Nuclear Weapons in South Asia (Surrey: Ashgate Publishing Ltd, 2011), pp.177-192.

58. "The Political-Military Background of the 2001-2002 Military Standoff: A Pakistani Perspective," in Zachary S. Davis, ed. The India-Pakistan Military Standoff: Crisis and Escalation in South Asia (United States: Palgrave Macmillan, March 2011), pp. 53-66.

59. "The Case of NATO Intervention in Kosovo and the Challenges to State Sovereignty," in Naveed Ahmad Tahir, ed. Humanitarian, Pre-emptive, Punitive and Political Intervention and State Sovereignty: Varying Political, Moral and Legal Standpoints Policy (Karachi: B.C.C.& T. Press, University of Karachi, June 2010), pp. 163-178.

60. "Role of Media, Public Opinion and Civil Society in Foreign Policy Making Process of Pakistan," in Moonis Ahmar, ed., Foreign Policy Making Process: A Case Study of Pakistan (Karachi: Bureau of Composition, Compilation & Translation, University of Karachi, 2009), pp. 95-109.

61. "The Euro-Mediterranean Partnership (EMP); An Attempt to Establish a Zone of Peace, Stability, Prosperity and Security, in Naveed Ahmed Tahir, ed., EU as an Emerging International Power: Its Middle East Policy (Karachi: B.C.C.& T. Press, University of Karachi, June 2009). pp, 95-112.

62. "Linkages between International Relations and Strategic Studies: A case study of Pakistan," in Moonis Ahmar, ed. International Relations Today: Theories, Methods and Areas of Research (Karachi: Bureau of Composition, Compilation & Translation, University of Karachi, 2009), pp. 101-124.

63. "Defense Policy of Pakistan: Imperative of Missiles," Syed Farooq Hasnat and Ahmed Farooqi, ed. Pakistan: Unresolved Issues of State & Society (Lahore: Vaneguard, 2008).

64. "Conflict Management Process in Afghanistan," in Moonis Ahmar, ed. Conflict Management Mechanisms and The Challenge of Peace, (Karachi: Bureau of Composition, 2008.

65. "Enhanced Defence Cooperation," in Hayatullah Khan Khattak, ed. US-Pakistan Strategic Partnership; a Track Two Process for Long-

Term Security Cooperation and Stability (Islamabad: ISSRA, NDU, 2007), pp. 81-103.

66. "The Induction of Ballistic Missiles: Impact on the Indo-Pak Nuclear Postures and Deterrence," in Pervaiz Iqbal Cheema, Brig. ® Muneer Mahmud, ed. Ballistic Missiles and South Asian Security (Islamabad: Asia Printers, 2007), pp.71- 87.

67. "Nuclear Risks in South Asia," in Dr. Umbreen Javaid, ed. Peace and Security in South Asia: Issues and Challenges (Lahore, Izharsons Printers, 2006), pp. 99-124.

68. "Assessment of Indian and Pakistani Nuclear Doctrines," in Pervaiz Iqbal Cheema and Imtiaz H. Bokhari, ed., Arms Race and Nuclear Developments in South Asia (Islamabad: Asia Printers, 2004).

69. "Dealing with nuclear weapons in South Asia: Safeguards, Verification and Monitoring," in Farooq Sobhan, ed., Strengthening Cooperation and Security in South Asia Post 9/11 (Dhaka: University Press Limited, 2004), pp. 35-53.

70. "Nuclear CBMs' Debate in South Asia: An Analysis", in Dr. Moonis Ahmar, ed. Paradigms of Conflict Resolution in South Asia (Dhaka: The University Press Limited, 2003), pp. 139-172.

71. "Kashmir: A Nuclear Flash Point?," in Rouben Azizian, ed, Nuclear Developments in South Asia and the Future of Global Arms Control: International, Regional and New Zealand Perspectives (New Zealand- Wellington: Centre for Strategic Studies, 2001), pp. 3-24.

72. "Globalization and its Effects on Pakistan's Security", Globalization and Security in South Asia, Proceedings of the Workshop at Bangladesh Institute of International and Strategic Studies (Dhaka, May 25-27, 1999).

73. "The Strategic Importance of the Persian Gulf in the Asian Politics: Pakistan's Perspective" The 12th International Conference on the Persian Gulf, on March 5-6, 2002. (Conference IPIS Journal, Tehran).

74. "Religious Radicalism/Extremism in Pakistan: Causes, Direction and Implication in South Asia, CNAS-HiPeC Discussion Series (Centre for Nepal and Asian Studies, Tribhuvan University, Kathmandu, Nepal and Hiroshima University, Hiroshima, Japan, December 2011).

75. "CD Agenda in 2011: Critical Appraisal," Research Report, No. 50, (London: South Asian Strategic Stability Institute, February 2011.
76. "Militarization and Weaponization of Space: A Critical Analysis," Research Report, No. 22 (London: South Asian Strategic Stability Institute, December 2008).
77. "Indo-U.S. Strategic Relationship & Pakistan Security," Research Report, No. 9 (London: South Asia Strategic Stability Institute, 2007).
78. "Arms Control: Risk Reduction Measures between India and Pakistan", Research Paper No. 1 (Bradford: South Asian Strategic Stability Unit, Department of Peace Studies, University of Bradford, June 2005).
79. "Terrorism" IPRI Paper, RPI/01 - written with Rafiuddin Ahmed, et. al. eds., December 20, 2001.

ALSO AVAILABLE FROM STRAND PUBLISHING UK LTD

The Strand Book Of Memorable Maxims - ISBN 9781907340000
The First Casualty by J Adam & MA Akbar - ISBN 9781907340031
The Challenge of Reality by Bashir Mahmood - ISBN 9781907340048
The Path Of The Gods by Joseph Geraci - ISBN 9781907340055
The Strand Book of International Poets 2010 – ISBN 9781907340062
The Assassins Code 1 by Christopher Chance -ISBN 9781907340123
Tragedy Of Deception by Humayun Niaz – ISBN 9781907340130
Marie Antoinette, Diana & Alexandra: The Third I by Alexandra Levin
The Box by Clive Parker-Sharp – ISBN 9781907340154
Storm Over Kabul by Imran Hanif – ISBN 9781907340208

All books are available to order online from Amazon.co.uk and Amazon.com, Kalahari.com, Play.com, Tesco.com, WH Smiths, Waterstones, Blackwells, Ingrams, Gardeners, from all good booksellers and direct from Strand quoting the ISBN number.

Follow us on Twitter: #strandpublishuk
Youtube: http://www.youtube.com/watch?v=xCa6XrkePNE
Facebook page: Strand Publishing UK Ltd
Pinterest, Google+

For more information about our books and services, visit:
http://www.strandpublishing.co.uk
email: info@strandpublishing.co.uk

Strand Publishing UK Ltd
Golden Cross House
8 Duncannon Street
Strand
London
WC2N 4JF
Registered in England & Wales Company Number 07034246

www.ingramcontent.com/pod-product-compliance
Lightning Source LLC
Chambersburg PA
CBHW051833090426
42736CB00011B/1788